CA2
ON
NR13
92G18

CELEBRATING 100 YEARS OF SERVICE 1892–1992

GAME WARDENS

MEN AND WOMEN IN CONSERVATION
JOE FISHER

DOCUMENT OFFICIELS

MAY 11 1992

GOVERNMENT PUBLICATIONS

ISBN 0-7729-9724-1

© 1992, Queen's Printer for Ontario
Printed in Ontario, Canada

You may purchase additional copies of this book
by calling either of the following two outlets:

        Ontario Federation of Anglers and Hunters
        Telephone   (705) 748-6324

        Ontario Government Bookstore, Publications Ontario
        Telephone   (416) 326-5300
        Toll free   1-800-668-9938

Cette publication est également disponible en français.

 Printed on recycled paper

Table of Contents

Message from The Duke of York iii

Minister's Introduction v

Chapter One: At the Forefront of Conservation............................1

Chapter Two: A Legacy of Plunder 5

Chapter Three: Five Men Strong and True 15

Chapter Four: Emergence of the Field Force..............................25

Chapter Five: The Post-War Era 31

Chapter Six: Give Us the Tools..41

Chapter Seven: Running the Gauntlet...57

Chapter Eight: The Poaching Menace 69

Chapter Nine: In School at Last...85

Chapter Ten: Helping Hands..95

Chapter Eleven: Four-Legged Deputies....................................107

Chapter Twelve: The Home Front..115

Chapter Thirteen: The Lighter Side 123

Chapter Fourteen: Looking Back (Carl Monk and John Macfie)....133

Chapter Fifteen: Last Words 145

Acknowledgements..149

The Warden's Century: A Timetable of Change 151

Glossary of Terms 156

BUCKINGHAM PALACE

The first centennial of Ontario's Conservation Officers in 1992 marks an historic and important event in the history of the Province of Ontario.

The role of the first game overseer was founded on dedication to the stewardship of Ontario's rich and varied natural resources based on the demand for efficient management, effective enforcement and the requirement for educating the public on the need for conservation. Much has changed over the last century but these common threads remain and today's 257 Conservation Officers can be justly proud of a tradition of which they are now the trustees. Their dedication has been unswerving and I congratulate them on their achievements.

I recall my former visits to Canada with great affection; and to the province of Ontario especially where I was fortunate to be at Lakefield College School and subsequently to visit Algonquin Park in 1986. I look forward to visiting Ontario in the future and for the present offer my best wishes to you on your centennial.

A message from His Royal Highness The Duke of York, to congratulate Ontario's Conservation Officers on their Centennial.

Minister's Introduction

This year we are celebrating a tradition that began a century ago. In 1892, the province of Ontario hired five game wardens; they were assigned the job of protecting wildlife across the entire province. Travelling on foot, by canoe, by dogsled and on horseback, they each patrolled, on average, an area almost three times the size of New Brunswick.

Those first five wardens established a proud tradition that continues today. Game wardens are known today as conservation officers—a name that reflects their broadened responsibility as guardians of Ontario's natural resources. Conservation officers are members of a team that includes, among others, biologists, foresters, aggregate inspectors and land technicians.

This book tells an important part of the history of the Ministry of Natural Resources—the history of Ontario's conservation officers. It is intended to be a fair and frank account. Since the book covers 100 years of social and political change, it reflects the ups and downs, and policy changes that are part of our history.

It is a rich history—sometimes humorous, sometimes stormy. Relations between conservation officers and policy-makers during the past century have at times been strained. But a common commitment to sound resource management has helped to form the strong and highly skilled team we have today.

Among the many individuals who have contributed in so many ways to this book, I would like to give special thanks to Mr. Carl Monk and Mr. John Macfie who, although retired from the ministry, have continued to dedicate their time and energy to ensuring this history is told.

I offer my congratulations to Ontario's conservation officers on their 100th anniversary. I know the province will continue to benefit from their experience and professionalism as we work together to conserve and protect Ontario's natural resources.

C.J. (Bud) Wildman

Chapter One: At the Forefront of Conservation

Long before the rise of the present "Green" movement, Ontario's conservation officers (C.O.s) were working to protect and enhance the natural resources of the province. It is fitting, then, that the officers' centenary should be celebrated in 1992, a year when the population at large is more keenly aware than ever of the vital importance of our lands and waters. This centennial history honours the guardians of a domain that stretches across more than one million square kilometres. These pages salute every serving warden since 1892 while paying tribute to the current field force of 257 officers and ninety other badge-carrying staff.

The first wardens were hardy part-timers who were paid $10 a month to protect Ontario's fish and wildlife. Likewise, the officers of the 1990s reflect a continuing awareness that all is not well with this generation's custody of the environment. Contemporary officers are professionals, well educated and rigorously trained. As guardians of the ecosystem, they apply some twenty-seven legal statutes while acting as roving ambassadors and resource managers.

The basic personality of C.O.s has changed little over the years. They tend to be a breed apart. They are dedicated and self-reliant with a passion for the

INSET: *The C.O.s of today, such as Paul Dreyer, radio information back to district offices from their patrol cars—faster than a day by dogsled or a slog by snowshoe.*

outdoors and a dislike of paperwork and bureaucracy. Once almost exclusively the products of rural families, they are now just as likely to hail from urban stock.

Their toughness and tenacity are legendary, qualities that are indispensable to people who often find themselves walking a fine line between conflicting interests. They also must be able to communicate well and see an issue from many different perspectives. C.O.s must ease tensions between

FIGURE 1-1
Wardens of yesteryear always paddled their own canoes. Officer Bill Ellerington, stationed at Dorset, was the focus of a feature by Toronto's Star Weekly in 1954.

hunters and naturalists or between trappers and animal rights activists. C.O.s must protect fish and wildlife while helping to provide hunting and fishing opportunities.

The C.O.s' mandate is to promote the idea of conservation while encouraging compliance with wide-ranging rules and regulations and enforcing them, if need be. It is recognized that the efficient officer must be everything from detective to philosopher, combining the skills of naturalist, trapper, botanist and good listener. While lawbreakers may be dealt with severely after being apprehended by a C.O., punishment is not the officer's objective.

Dorset C.O. Bill Ellerington put it this way in an interview with Toronto's *Star Weekly* in 1954: "I'm not here to punish people. I'm here to conserve wildlife. If I can show someone the errors of their ways, fine. If I can't, then I have to turn the job over to the courts. People just have to learn that conservation is necessary. The more wildlife, the more tourists, the more prosperity. Everyone has an interest in this thing if they can be made to realize it. My job is to make it clear to them one way or another."

C.O.s are classified differently by various resource users. From "Gamey" or "Woodpecker Sheriff" to "Weass Ougamow" (Cree for "Meat Boss") to the most ordinary yet most common "Fish Cop," nicknames for officers reflect the job's unbroken association with the wild.

In the big cities of southern Ontario, C.O.s are not so well known and have been mistakenly identified as cabbies, bus drivers and "green hornets." Although in use since 1948, the official term "conservation officer" is not always immediately recognizable. "But when we say 'game warden,'" offered officer coordinator Rick Stankiewicz, "everyone understands." Accordingly, in order to gain the widest possible audience, this book is titled *Game Wardens*.

One hundred years of wardens' exploits amount to no ordinary tale. It is a narrative of danger and adversity, of challenge and humour, of perseverance and big-heartedness. The chronicle starts before the first wardens were appointed, when the landscape of Ontario had yet to feel the rough and often thoughtless hands of newcomers.

Chapter Two: A Legacy of Plunder

Once upon a time, long before dire necessity dictated the hiring of Ontario's first game wardens, an almost unbroken forest stretched from Lake Erie's shoreline north to the Hudson Bay lowlands. A wide variety of wildlife inhabited this uncharted wilderness; the lakes, rivers and streams teemed with fish. Algonquian-, Iroquoian- and Siouan-speaking peoples lived off the land, neither questioning nor encroaching upon nature's ability to sustain them. Here and there, some Iroquoian villages contained several thousand people.

Then came the Europeans. But mercifully, at least initially, the majesty of the forest held sway. Several strangers to the New World wrote lyrically of the magnificence they encountered. Anna Jameson, after a sightseeing tour of what was to become southwestern Ontario, observed in 1837: "No one who has a single atom of imagination can travel through these forest roads of Canada without being strongly impressed and excited. The seemingly interminable line of trees before you; the boundless wilderness around; the mysterious depths amid the multitudinous foliage where foot of man hath never penetrated...."

That same year, Donald Wilkie commented on "the unnatural and powerful silence" of the densely wooded landscape in *Sketches of a Summer Trip* and Richard Bonnycastle in *The Canadas in 1841* voiced feelings of "horror" inspired by the infinite loneliness of the forest.

Ontario's population grew very quickly in the eighteenth century. Loyalists seeking refuge from the battles for independence in the U.S. colonies

LEFT: *In the early days, in spite of laws to limit the hunting season of deer and fur-bearing animals, there was no limit to the number of animals taken in season. Hunting clubs, such as the Heart Lake club pictured here in 1906, were popular in the Ontario wilderness.*

National Archives of Canada / PA-29169

moved into the southern reaches of the province, followed by settlers from Great Britain and other European nations. Between 1763 and 1824, immigrants responding to the promise of over 5 million hectares of land sent the population soaring to 150,000. By 1838, that number had more than doubled to 400,000.

Surveyors flocked into the hinterland, dividing and sub-dividing, allocating townships and concessions. So sacrosanct was their quest to dissect the wilderness that, for a while, the crime of removing or defacing a survey post was punishable by death. On the other hand, the devastation of primeval forest and the wholesale destruction of fish and game were considered to be perfectly acceptable—in fact, a goal to be achieved. Why? Because the natural resources of Ontario were thought to be inexhaustibly abundant and self-replenishing—and of course, the creation of farms from the wilderness required the clearing of forested lands.

As Canada struggled towards nationhood, this destruction of the wild was long and unrelenting. Many people left behind lives of caution and restraint and armed themselves with guns, nets and axes to carve out a new existence and create a new land out of the wilderness.

Initially, few rules controlled the harvest of fish and wildlife. The first game law was decreed by General Thomas Gage, the military governor of Montreal, who in 1762 proclaimed an annual closed

FIGURE 2-1
Ontario's forests were still a major source of income at the turn of the century. This logging operation was at Diver.

season on "partridges," or ruffed grouse, from March 15 to July 15.

The decree stemmed from awareness that the birds were "being reduced from day to day by pursuit...during their mating periods." The stiff penalty of "one hundred livres"—roughly £5 or $25—was to be shared equally between the poor of the parish in which the crime took place and whoever turned in the offending hunter. No one was charged

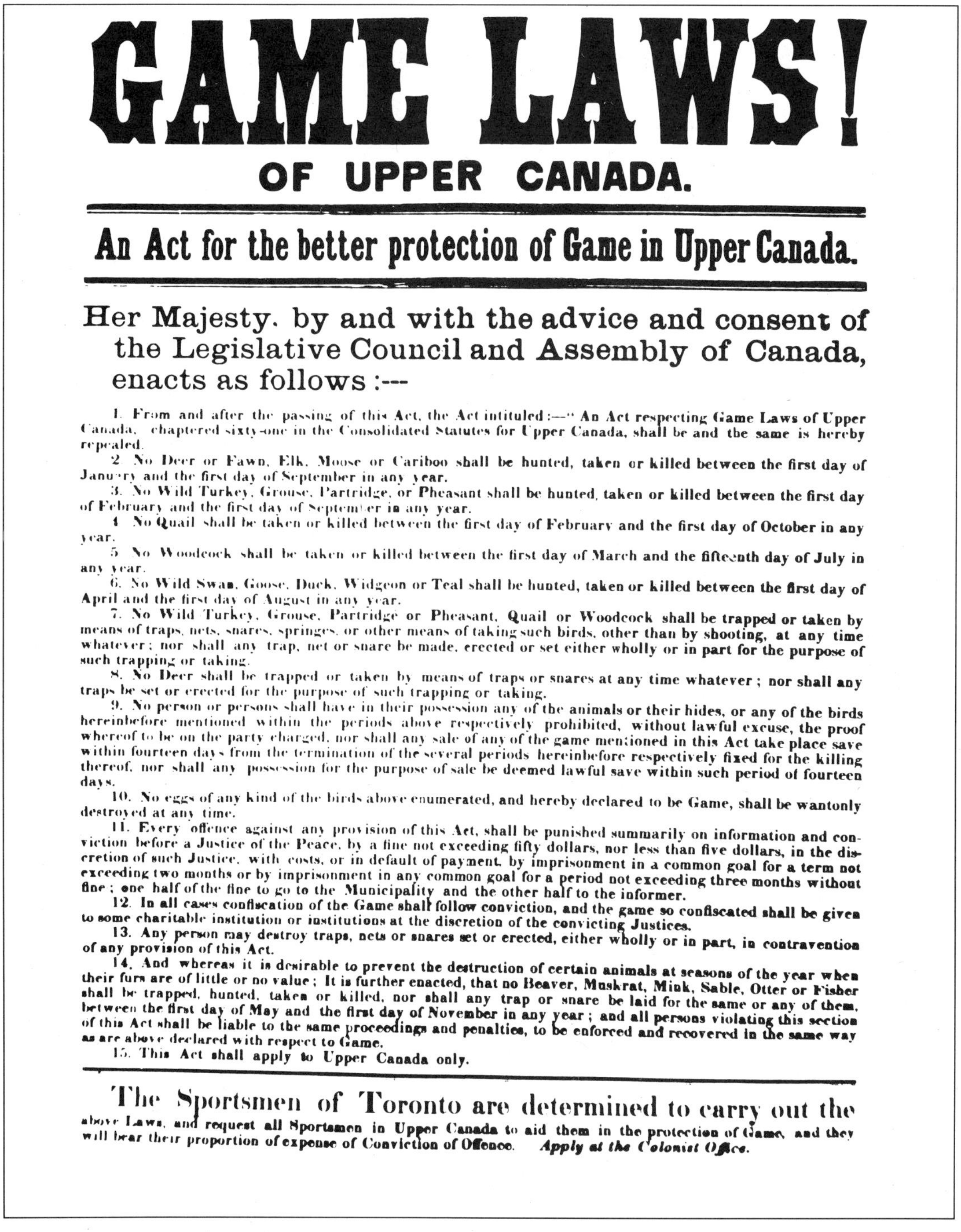

FIGURE 2-2
An 1860 poster proclaiming the game laws of Upper Canada. Few heeded the statutes.

GAME LAWS!
OF UPPER CANADA.

An Act for the better protection of Game in Upper Canada.

Her Majesty, by and with the advice and consent of the Legislative Council and Assembly of Canada, enacts as follows :—

1. From and after the passing of this Act, the Act intituled :—" An Act respecting Game Laws of Upper Canada, chaptered sixty-one in the Consolidated Statutes for Upper Canada, shall be and the same is hereby repealed.
2. No Deer or Fawn, Elk, Moose or Cariboo shall be hunted, taken or killed between the first day of January and the first day of September in any year.
3. No Wild Turkey, Grouse, Partridge, or Pheasant shall be hunted, taken or killed between the first day of February and the first day of September in any year.
4. No Quail shall be taken or killed between the first day of February and the first day of October in any year.
5. No Woodcock shall be taken or killed between the first day of March and the fifteenth day of July in any year.
6. No Wild Swan, Goose, Duck, Widgeon or Teal shall be hunted, taken or killed between the first day of April and the first day of August in any year.
7. No Wild Turkey, Grouse, Partridge or Pheasant, Quail or Woodcock shall be trapped or taken by means of traps, nets, snares, springes, or other means of taking such birds, other than by shooting, at any time whatever ; nor shall any trap, net or snare be made, erected or set either wholly or in part for the purpose of such trapping or taking.
8. No Deer shall be trapped or taken by means of traps or snares at any time whatever ; nor shall any traps be set or erected for the purpose of such trapping or taking.
9. No person or persons shall have in their possession any of the animals or their hides, or any of the birds hereinbefore mentioned within the periods above respectively prohibited, without lawful excuse, the proof whereof to be on the party charged, nor shall any sale of any of the game mentioned in this Act take place save within fourteen days from the termination of the several periods hereinbefore respectively fixed for the killing thereof, nor shall any possession for the purpose of sale be deemed lawful save within such period of fourteen days.
10. No eggs of any kind of the birds above enumerated, and hereby declared to be Game, shall be wantonly destroyed at any time.
11. Every offence against any provision of this Act, shall be punished summarily on information and conviction before a Justice of the Peace, by a fine not exceeding fifty dollars, nor less than five dollars, in the discretion of such Justice, with costs, or in default of payment, by imprisonment in a common goal for a term not exceeding two months or by imprisonment in any common goal for a period not exceeding three months without fine ; one half of the fine to go to the Municipality and the other half to the informer.
12. In all cases confiscation of the Game shall follow conviction, and the game so confiscated shall be given to some charitable institution or institutions at the discretion of the convicting Justices.
13. Any person may destroy traps, nets or snares set or erected, either wholly or in part, in contravention of any provision of this Act.
14. And whereas it is desirable to prevent the destruction of certain animals at seasons of the year when their furs are of little or no value ; It is further enacted, that no Beaver, Muskrat, Mink, Sable, Otter or Fisher shall be trapped, hunted, taken or killed, nor shall any trap or snare be laid for the same or any of them, between the first day of May and the first day of November in any year ; and all persons violating this section of this Act shall be liable to the same proceedings and penalties, to be enforced and recovered in the same way as are above declared with respect to Game.
15. This Act shall apply to Upper Canada only.

The Sportsmen of Toronto are determined to carry out the
above Laws, and request all Sportsmen in Upper Canada to aid them in the protection of Game, and they will bear their proportion of expense of Conviction of Offence. *Apply at the Colonist Office.*

with enforcing the law, its upkeep relying entirely upon "the informant"—anyone who might be willing to go in for a little part-time bounty hunting.

The decline in the Atlantic salmon runs of Lake Ontario hastened The Act for the Preservation of Salmon in 1807. Although this statute prohibited the "setting of any net or nets…to take any salmon, or salmon fry, in river or creek," the utter lack of enforcement rendered the legislation quite worthless. Several years later, according to a federal fisheries report, people were descending greedily on spawning salmon at Wilmot Creek, which ran into Lake Ontario: "…men killed them with clubs and pitchforks, women seined them with flannel petticoats, and settlers bought and paid for farms and built houses from the sale of salmon. Later, they were taken by nets and spears, over 1,000 being often caught in the course of one night."

By 1856, the exploitation of all kinds of fish had reached such proportions that Joseph Cauchon, commissioner of Crown Lands for Upper and Lower Canada, cried out in his annual report for enforcement officers to be installed "for the preservation of our fisheries." A Fisheries Act was passed prohibiting harmful fishing practices such as the spearing of salmon by torchlight, as well as providing for the appointment of federal fishery overseers to enforce the statute by search and seizure.

Even this was insufficient to reverse the plunder by either residents or visitors; Upper Canada was quickly developing a reputation as a hunting and fishing paradise.

Violence was an everyday hazard to those wardens who placed themselves between the resources and those who set out to plunder them. "We are completely at the mercy of this class of lawless men," John McCuaig, superintendent of fisheries for Upper Canada, had warned ominously in his annual report for 1859. He pointed out the impossibility of getting local people to inform against illegal fishing "for fear of consequences to themselves and property." Moreover, this was a desperately gloomy era for the provincial fisheries. "Many of the rivers which once abounded with the choicest fish are now entirely or almost forsaken," McCuaig's report intoned.

Four years later, William Gibbard, fishery overseer for the district of Lake Huron and Superior, became Ontario's first recorded martyr to the cause of conservation. He was bludgeoned to death aboard the steamer *Ploughboy* while pursuing his duty as a fishery overseer; his bruised and lacerated body was found floating in the water near Manitoulin Island. Gibbard's killers were never brought to justice.

By 1883—despite Samuel Wilmot's efforts to turn the tide by administering, at Newcastle, the first government fish hatchery in the western

> **[William Gibbard] was bludgeoned to death aboard the steamer *Ploughboy* while pursuing his duty as a fishery overseer; his bruised and lacerated body was found floating in the water near Manitoulin Island. Gibbard's killers were never brought to justice.**

hemisphere—Atlantic salmon in Lake Ontario was extinct. Aiding and abetting the excessive slaughter, mill dams along the rivers had impeded the spawning runs, and dams and factories had resulted in the loss of spawning beds. This mournful predicament was repeated in the 1890s when the Lake Erie sturgeon—once so common that farm labourers begged their employers *not* to feed them the fish on a daily basis—declined and all but disappeared because of over-exploitation.

While laws on the statute books failed to save the salmon and the sturgeon, similar paper measures were aimed at the protection of game. In 1821, when deer became much less plentiful, a closed season was established between January 10 and July 1. A penalty of £2 was levied against would-be poachers—a sum considerably less than the £5 General Gage had demanded fifty-nine years earlier for every grouse shot out-of-season in Lower Canada.

In 1839, the first general game law for Upper Canada introduced shorter open seasons for all classes of game and ruled that "no person shall hunt or shoot or go out with a gun in the quest of any deer or other wild animal or wild fowl on the Lord's Day."

In 1868, the year after confederation, this game law became a provincial statute and the big game season was clipped to three months, from September 1 to December 1. The sale of game was declared illegal fourteen days after the season closing date and the taking or destruction of game bird eggs was prohibited. Penalties of pounds and shillings gave way to

While laws on the statute books failed to save the salmon and the sturgeon, similar paper measures were aimed at the protection of game.

FIGURE 2-3
Canoe travel in Algonquin Park gave easy access to the wilderness, but it did have its upsets. Cy Warman and Charles Young of the Cornwall Freeholder drag their sodden canoe to shore after one such mishap in Algonquin Park Lake sometime between 1911 and 1913.
National Archives of Canada / C-54533

fines of $2 to $25 for each head of game taken illegally.

The first law to protect fur-bearing animals was introduced in 1860. An Act Respecting Game Laws in Upper Canada ruled that no beaver, muskrat, mink, sable, otter or fisher shall be trapped, hunted, taken or killed, nor any trap or snare laid for any of them between May 1 and November 1 in any year.

The laws sounded innovative and far-seeing, but there were no limits on the numbers of animals and birds that could be taken during open seasons. The result was that the slaughter of animals, birds and fish proceeded as if legislation did not exist. Wildlife populations shrank and shrank.

Meanwhile, the devastation of the forests continued. Clearing of land for agriculture continued to be encouraged with free grants of land. Additionally, commercial tree harvest was promoted. The timber trade was a treasure trove of governmental revenue and, although enforcement of the game and fish laws was yet to be undertaken, travelling inspectors or "woods rangers" were despatched to lumber camps to verify the measurements of all timber cut and the amount of dues payable. Such attention to detail ensured that Ontario's forests yielded as much cash annually for the public purse as all the forests of Upper and Lower Canada combined had contributed in the most affluent pre-confederation years.

> **The impact of forest removal was not only on the land. In 1860, after many spawning beds had been covered with sawmill waste, mill detritus was banned from rivers and streams.**

The impact of forest removal was not only on the land. In 1860, after many spawning beds had been covered with sawmill waste, mill detritus was banned from rivers and streams. Five years later, the prohibition against discharged materials was extended to lime, chemicals, drugs, poisonous matter, dead fish or any other "deleterious substance." However, on the few occasions when the captains of industry were charged and convicted, the penalty was small. In 1876, for example, a mill owner was fined $8 and costs for allowing sawdust and mill rubbish to fall from his mill into a creek in the township of Bedford.

When the lumber industry entered a prolonged depression in the late 1870s, politicians, civil servants and mill owners alike were forced to reconsider their endorsement of unbridled consumption. For the first time, the principle of "conservation" was invoked by opponents to a massive auction sale of timber berths north of Lake Huron. It was claimed that the long-term interests of the people of the province were being sacrificed to the brief, commercial advantage of a few wealthy merchants.

Caught in a maelstrom of changing attitudes, the Department of Crown Lands—an early forerunner of the Ministry of Natural Resources—began a radical transformation from being the handmaiden of industry to managing the resources of the province for everyone's benefit. Gradually, the provincial government surrendered its exploitive stance in order to undertake the trusteeship of everything renewable in the natural world.

As this reformation took shape, an obscure clerk named Alexander Kirkwood in the Crown Lands Department had a revolutionary idea: to set aside a vast area of wilderness where trees, plants and wildlife would be protected and conserved for the enjoyment of future generations. Kirkwood's brainchild, received unenthusiastically at first, would soon emerge in 1893 as Algonquin Park.

The new environmental perspective that was emerging was fuelled by the concerns of sports enthusiasts and naturalists who had grown fretful at the scarcity of wildlife. Whole species were beginning to disappear in Ontario. The eastern sub-species of elk, for example, was seen no more after 1875, the demise of the cougar followed during the 1880s, and the passenger pigeon and the wild turkey disappeared soon afterwards. Perhaps the loss of the passenger pigeon was most keenly felt because its numbers had been so great. As recently as 1838, R. Montgomery Martin in the *History, Statistics and Geography of Upper and Lower Canada* had told how flocks of this beautiful bird of blue plumage would "darken the sky for miles when annually migrating towards the north."

A crisis was in the making and it came as no surprise when a ten-member Royal Commission, the Ontario Fish and Game Commission, was set up in 1890 under the chairship of Dr. G.A. MacCallum to inquire into the state of game and fish in the province. Response was immediate and overwhelming to the Commission's notice of a questionnaire to be completed by anyone interested in the "protection, preservation and propagation" of wildlife. Letters poured in from neighbouring U.S. states as well as from all parts of the province. When the views of everyone from locksmiths to carriage makers, from farmers to physicians, had been examined, the Commission issued an interim report that reflected a population just as divided as today.

"The true sportsmen, and those desirous of seeing the province restocked with game and fish, have invariably expressed a willingness to sink all smaller considerations in order that the most good might be done," the report stated. "But others with narrower minds have given such answers as are applicable only to their own cases; some of them going so far as to say that no steps of any kind should be taken to preserve the game and fish in Ontario, because these were already scarce and might as well be used up by the present generation."

Also, more than 280 people testified before the travelling Commission, venting their opinions on everything from: "Should foreigners be allowed to shoot game birds in Ontario?" to "Should pioneer settlers be allowed to take fish by legal methods at all seasons for their family food?"

When all witnesses had been heard, the Commission delivered a withering indictment of a province that teetered on the brink of annihilating its game and fish populations. "On all sides, from every quarter, has been heard the same sickening tale of merciless, ruthless and remorseless slaughter," the commissioners declared. "Where but a few years ago, game was plentiful, it is hardly now to be found, and there is a great danger that, as in the case of the buffalo, even those animals which have been so numerous as to be looked upon with contempt, will soon become extinct."

The report added: "The extent to which the game birds of the province are being slaughtered for exportation to the United States is almost incredible. Boys are hired by stage-drivers, train-hands, commission merchants and others to bring in as large a supply as possible, and the extermination goes on incessantly."

The clearing of the land, the cutting down of the forests, the introduction of the railways, the use of dynamite and nets as well as the "indiscriminate hunting of the human assassin" had all contributed to what the Commission called a "deplorable state of affairs." While protective laws were in place, "the laws touching upon game and fish [were] everywhere left to be disregarded, unless utilized by informers for their own rather than the public good."

The commissioners went on to make a series of sweeping recommendations. These included:
- a ban on shooting of deer for five years in southwestern Ontario;
- a ban on all trapping of beaver, otter and fisher for five years;
- the prohibition of all exports of game from Ontario; and
- a $25 licence for "foreign sportsmen" wishing to hunt and fish during the open season.

The most important long-term recommendation of all was an oft-repeated call for a provincial force of game and fish wardens who would provide teeth for what had been lifeless legislation. Lacking a serious-minded enforcement team, Ontario was said to have fallen behind "some of the least civilized states and territories."

Certainly, there were a small number of federal and provincial fishery overseers, but the Commission noted that "the majority of them take little, if any, pains to prohibit illegal fishing and to protect the valuable stock entrusted to their care." Provincial statutes also provided for the appointment of "game inspectors" but, by all accounts, they too were ineffective.

A.D. Stewart, who was secretary of the Ontario Game and Fish Commission, derided these token inspectors who, when infrequently appointed, were paid an annual salary of $40. He told an international committee in

Rochester on November 10, 1891, that the inspectors, not wishing to incur the ill-will of neighbours, "very wisely pocketed the $40 a year and did nothing."

Speaking of Ontario's wildlife at large, he went on: "There is no protection, and it simply arises from that fact that it has been everybody's business and nobody's business in particular to enforce the laws."

Fortunately for the heirs of Ontario's natural resources, the years of laxness and indifference were almost over. A.D. Stewart himself would soon be appointed chief warden of a small but determined force charged with calling a halt to the ransacking of the land and waters. The history of Ontario's conservation officers, as we know them today, was about to begin.

Chapter Three: Five Men Strong and True

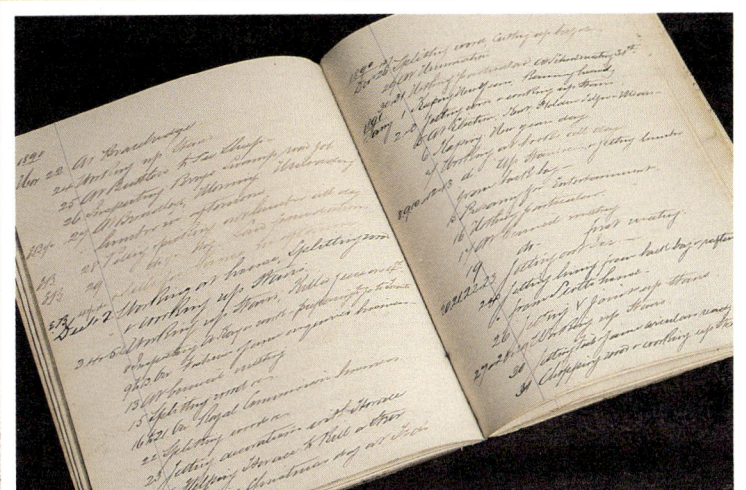

Ontario's first game wardens were hardy, thick-skinned and relentlessly optimistic. They had to be. There were only five of them, a tiny human bulwark placed defiantly between a portfolio of new game laws and a vast province of pioneers thoroughly accustomed to hunting and fishing wherever, whenever and however they pleased.

The five men who stepped up to accept the daunting challenge of official protectors must have known they were attempting more than they could possibly hope to accomplish. They had no idea that they were founding a movement that—over the course of a century—would grow into a well-equipped force of more than 250 conservation officers charged with safeguarding Ontario's natural resources.

The original five men were appointed under the 1892 Act for the Protection of Game and Fur-Bearing Animals, which converted into law many of the recommendations made by the Game and Fish Commission. A.D. Stewart (the Commission secretary) of Hamilton was named chief warden. His part-time enforcers were: John H. Willmott of Beaumaris; H.K. Smith of Belleville; John A. Gill of Dunnville and Charles Quallins of Leamington. No one cared to mention that their task was physically impossible. Nonetheless, some much-needed help was supplied by 392 deputy wardens who,

INSET: *Diary recorded by John Willmott.*
LEFT: *A route map used by John Willmott to help navigate the Muskoka Lakes—a small portion of his vast patrol area.*

FIGURE 3-1
One of the five men strong and true: Game warden John Willmott of Beaumaris who, starting in 1892, served for more than twenty years. An obituary in the Bracebridge Gazette *praised his "judicial mind unwarped by considerations other than rendering justice to all."*

though unpaid, received one-half of fines—ranging from $20 to $50—collected from offenders who were convicted on their testimony.

The four wardens in the field were originally vested with the powers of prosecutor and judge so that they could convict "on view." Their labours were rewarded with a monthly salary of $10, a sum readily admitted as inadequate by the Commission, which blamed the government for failing to allocate sufficient funds. Observed Chief Warden Stewart: "It will be a surprise to the citizens of the province when they learn that these officers have given up their time...in some cases to the utter ruin of their private business."

The new Act clamped down hard in a last-ditch bid to save the declining wildlife of the province. Deer hunting was limited to fifteen days in November; all hunting of moose and caribou was forbidden until 1895; a ban on the slaughter of wild turkeys, beaver, otter and fisher was extended until 1897; the purchase and sale of quail, snipe, wild turkey, woodcock and partridge was banned outright.

To help pay for the new force of wardens, the cost of a non-resident hunting licence leapt from $10 to $25. In 1892, just fifty-six of these licences were sold—a minute fraction of the 33,816 sold in 1988. There was also a strange wrinkle in the fine print accompanying the legislation. The law insisted these licences must be produced by their owners "at all times and as often as requested" before any inquiring Ontario resident—hardly an inducement to goodwill from visiting hunters!

The first annual report of the Ontario Board of Game Commissioners told how the earliest game wardens were at the forefront of an "energetic effort" aimed at halting the "ruthless and indiscriminate destruction" of the province's wildlife. Finding that the public suffered from "the most lamentable ignorance" concerning the game and fishery laws, the Board instigated a program of mass education to inform people about the closed seasons for various forms of wildlife as well as the penalties for breaking the rules.

Bearing instructions that they be prominently displayed, 20,000 copies of the laws mounted on large cardboard sheets and another 10,000 in pamphlet form were sent across the province to justices of the peace, magistrates, postmasters, custom house officers, railway agents, newspaper editors and telegraph agents. Each deputy warden, too, received a parcel of literature for local distribution so that, in the words of the board's annual report for 1892, "the poachers and the pot-hunters awoke to the fact that at last they were likely to be brought to book for their nefarious practices."

And so the wardens went to work armed with a government badge but precious little else. They were expected to arm and dress themselves appropriately (there were no uniforms or issued firearms in those days) and travel by train, by horse or by carriage to the limits of civilization, then hike through the bush as far as their legs would carry them. In winter, they might have the use of snowshoes or a dogsled. In summer, they would navigate the lakes and rivers by rowboat or canoe.

They were alone. They were very few. They were poorly paid and ill-equipped. Their arena of operations stretched as far as the wilderness itself. Considering these difficulties—to say nothing of having to deal with belligerent offenders—their efforts yielded results that were not only remarkable, but remarkably rapid.

By the end of the first year, A.D. Stewart was telling his commissioners with pride that not one-quarter of the game slaughtered in previous seasons had been killed over the past year. "There is no manner of doubt," he enthused, "that the game and fish have been protected during this past season as they have never been protected before in the history of Ontario."

Board chair, Dr. G.A. MacCallum congratulated the wardens on the "thorough manner" in which their work had been done. "They have proved themselves to be intelligent, active, and zealous…" he declared. Two years later, Dr. MacCallum announced that the "wanton slaughter" of game and fish had for the most part ceased. In 1895, he applauded the wardens for being "unremitting in their efforts to enforce the provisions of the game and fish laws, thus earning directly for the people of the province many times their salary."

The wardens drafted reports indicating a drastic reduction in slaughtered animals. Deer, particularly, appeared to be making a comeback. "It is reported on all hands," noted warden H.K. Smith of Belleville, "that deer are quite numerous in the various localities frequented by hunters, showing that they have not been disturbed to anything like the same extent as in previous seasons."

The wardens' unrealistically large patrol areas were already posing problems.

Those original observations were perhaps overly optimistic, and fisheries remained largely unprotected. The wardens' unrealistically large patrol areas were already posing problems. "I may say," Smith remarked, "that the guardianship of the inland waters is not as satisfactory as I could wish; it happens that many of the lakes on which…illegal practices are indulged in are considerable distances from settlements and consequently beyond the immediate supervision of any of our deputies."

In any case, there were trying times in store for any game warden endeavouring to enforce the fisheries laws. The federal government and the province were fighting for control of the resource and many charges were fought successfully on the grounds that the province had no say in the matter.

Checking non-resident hunting licences, wardens found themselves on a more solid legal foundation. In 1893, warden Charles Quallins encountered a variety of schemes hatched by non-resident hunters to avoid paying the $25 licence fee. Some visitors, he discovered, would borrow the guns of Canadian friends, then pose as Canadians; others would buy one licence and share it among their pals. Frustrated by this deception, Quallins urged specific action to tighten up the Act.

A warden's day could be very long. John Gill wrote in his report for 1893 that he "had often to be on the ground between three and four in the morning in certain places and localities where [he] was not expected… " so that he could catch illegal hunters in the act—something he managed to do with impressive regularity.

With one exception, very little is known about the lifestyles and personalities of the first wardens. That exception is John Harry Willmott, warden for the Muskoka Lakes, whose daughter-in-law, Bernice Willmott, and grandson John Willmott Anderson, still live in the tiny settlement of Beaumaris (pop. 15) where J.H.W. was based for more than forty years.

A heavy-set, mustachioed gentleman known locally as "The Guv'nor," John Willmott was born in Cheshire, England, on April 4, 1844. Adventurous by nature, he left his native land as a young man and headed for South America on a mission for the Bank of England. In Buenos Aires, he became manager of one of the country's largest cattle ranching companies. Striking north in due course, he spent time in New York and other U.S. cities before settling in Chatham, Ontario.

From Chatham, Willmott took a trip in 1872 through the much-heralded Muskoka Lakes and was so impressed that he decided to settle there. He soon married a local girl, Catherine McMahon, and purchased Tondern Island for $500 in partnership with his brother-in-law, Edward Prowse. On Tondern Island, which is eight kilometres around, Willmott built a one-storey log cabin of stout pine logs where all nine of his children were born. Over the years, the cabin was progressively extended into a large and attractive residence that, though now a real-estate office, still commands a grand view of Lake Muskoka.

FIGURE 3-2
Sports enthusiasts gather around an evening camp fire to share stories of the day's events in Temagmi District, 1897.

Ellis W.H. (Dr.) / National Archives of Canada / PA-121269

Willmott was principally a farmer but he also sold supplies from his home and, around 1898, opened a general store that remains in operation today. Always interested in public affairs, he served the township of Monck, first as councillor and later as reeve.

Willmott entered the rough and tumble existence of a game warden relatively late in life. He was forty-eight years old when hired by the Board of Game Commissioners to enforce the game laws. A member of the board himself for two years, he had already been working for several years as a part-time federal fisheries overseer and, in 1899, would also be appointed, when jurisdiction shifted, as a provincial fishery overseer.

Game warden, fishery overseer, farmer, storeowner, politician and father of nine, Willmott must have been hard pressed for relaxation time, although we do know that he was an avid stamp collector.

In later years, he sold—for $17,000—some sheep pasture that would become nine holes of the eighteen-hole Beaumaris golf course. This, too, is very much a going concern today.

Bernice Willmott, who was married to the late Norman Willmott, the last of Willmott's offspring, never knew her father-in-law. But she has several keepsakes once owned by him—his diaries, his route map through the Muskoka Lakes (marking portages, waterfalls and lumber camps), his roll-top desk and a trio of rye, gin and scotch decanters enclosed in a silver container. The hardback diaries, crammed with an almost illegible pen-and-ink scrawl, give brief accounts of clearing back pastures, travelling to Bracebridge to testify against offenders, ploughing, lambing and digging potatoes.

> **The hardback diaries, crammed with an almost illegible pen-and-ink scrawl, give brief accounts of clearing back pastures, travelling to Bracebridge to testify against offenders, ploughing, lambing and digging potatoes.**

"John Willmott was a very popular man who worked very hard and liked the nice things in life," said Bernice, who lives just a stone's throw from the house that Willmott built. One of the things he liked was whisky. For years, or so the story goes, the letters "O.B.J." were inscribed on his monthly expense accounts sent to Queen's Park. Eventually, a government accountant asked about the significance of this inscription. John Willmott explained that the letters stood for "Oh Be Joyful!"—his code for the bottle of whisky that would regularly accompany him on long patrols through the Muskoka Lakes.

"I have endeavoured to curtail expenses as much as possible," he wrote, "but on account of these districts being so extensive, and most of the travel being necessarily by horse conveyance, the expenses are unavoidably high."

Many stories have been passed down through the family describing the old man's exploits as a warden. Bernice tells of the time he was inspecting a local house whose inhabitants were known to be poachers. As Willmott entered the house, a woman was waiting for him poised with a hatchet held high and menacingly. After much verbal entreaty, Willmott managed to persuade the woman to surrender the weapon.

In 1896, Willmott testified to winning fifteen convictions out of twenty-two cases. But the Guv'nor didn't always win the day. Once, when Willmott seized nets from anglers who were contravening the laws, he draped the captured nets over a nearby roof to dry and went home for the night. Next morning, the nets were gone, never to be seen again.

Perhaps the most amusing tale of all tells how Willmott met the local priest returning by boat from Mortimer's Point where he had conducted a service at St. Anne's Church. Willmott happened to know that some Mortimer's Point residents had been slaughtering moose, and the bulging luggage in the boat edging towards the Beaumaris dock caused him to suspect the parishioners had bestowed illicit gifts upon their cleric. "Good morning, Father," Willmott greeted the priest. "May I carry your bags?"

In 1894—soon after wardens' salaries were increased from $120 to $400 a year—warden John Gill was instructed to help John Willmott enforce the game laws during deer season in the Muskokas. Gill's report painted a picture of pastoral delight, recounting that the two wardens rowed for nine miles* down the Muskoka River before reaching the camp of a hunter "who kindly invited us to partake of a portion of his venison and other good things, and allowed us to share his tent and blankets with him for the night."

The report continued: "This gentleman had shot two deer, and his guide,

> Willmott happened to know that some Mortimer's Point residents had been slaughtering moose, and the bulging luggage in the boat edging towards the Beaumaris dock caused him to suspect the parishioners had bestowed illicit gifts upon their cleric.

FIGURE 3-3
Sports hunters load their take onto railway baggage cars to transport it home from the Haliburton railway station in 1889.

National Archives of Canada / RD-39

* 1.6 kilometres = 1 mile

FIGURE 3-4
Warden John Willmott's patrol boat Meenagha, *circa 1910.*

one, and they were trying to capture a bear. This done he would strike for his home in Ohio satisfied that he had got more than $25 worth of sport out of his licence.

"On my return home I found the train crowded with returning sportsmen, including dogs and catch of game. The stench arising from the carcasses was almost unbearable. I talked with all the parties on the train and counted the deer claimed by each, and found all well."

In 1893, when the province was officially divided into five wardens' zones, Willmott's region was designated as the districts of Algoma, Muskoka, Nipissing, Parry Sound and the County of Simcoe—a massive patrol area for a man equipped with little more than a rowboat! In 1910, however, Willmott was granted the use of a motorized open wooden boat, five-and-a-half metres in length, complete with canopy, called *Meenagha*.

Though into middle age before signing on as a warden, John Harry Willmott outlasted his fellow founding officers. By 1907, he was the only original member of the enforcement service still on patrol. Exactly when Willmott retired is not known, but it is thought he persevered into his late sixties. He died in 1916, at the age of seventy-two, after suffering from a lengthy illness. Willmott's obituary in the *Bracebridge Gazette* pays tribute to the long-standing and efficient service of a warden who covered "all the northern districts." He did his job, said the *Gazette*, with rare tact and judgement, "exercising a judicial mind unwarped by considerations other than rendering justice to all."

Many were the tests and privations facing the early wardens, not the least of these being the fraudulent behaviour of some people charged with violations. Chief Warden A.D. Stewart told how certain offenders waited until summoned for trial and then, ignoring the fact that the law had been set in motion, made their way in company with an accomplice to a friendly magistrate. The accomplice, expecting to receive half the fine upon conviction, would give bogus evidence against his friend, and the friendly magistrate would then proceed to inflict the lowest possible fine.

When the fine was paid, the accomplice promptly handed over his share to the defendant and, in this way, the offender emerged with a nominal penalty. Even more discomfitting than this miscarriage of justice, however, was the unfortunate predicament in which the arresting warden would then find himself. In the words of A.D. Stewart: "When the original case is called for trial, the offender produces a record of his conviction, and as he cannot be tried twice, the constable is saddled with heavy costs and is out of pocket, whilst the lawbreakers for miles around laugh him to scorn and set to work again to outwit him if possible."

> In 1898, after a protracted legal wrangle, Ontario won jurisdiction over the fisheries of the province from the federal government. Immediately afterwards, ninety-four provincial fishery overseers were appointed to enforce the fisheries laws.

By 1906, the initial euphoria over the supposed victory against threats posed to Ontario's wildlife had evaporated. The Board of Commissioners reported soberly that a special investigation of conditions prevailing in different parts of the province had made it plain that the province's live resources were not sufficiently protected after all. "No species of game is increasing and many are in danger of extinction," commented chair H.S. Osler.

The board's conclusion was that laws merely establishing closed seasons were inadequate. It was felt the law must also contain provisions to restrict the amount of game taken each year—a philosophy that was soon to be adopted for decades to come.

To ready itself for the challenges ahead, the wardens' administration required an overhaul to merge the role of warden with that of fishery overseer. (John Willmott, it must be noted, had managed both jobs side by side for several years.)

In 1898, after a protracted legal wrangle, Ontario won jurisdiction over the fisheries of the province from the federal government. Immediately afterwards, ninety-four provincial fishery overseers were appointed to enforce the fisheries laws. By 1905, however, the Board of Game Commissioners was expressing dismay at the "unnecessary waste of energy and money" in running separate organizations to enforce the game and fish laws.

"Why not unite the jobs of fishery overseer and deputy warden?" demanded the commissioners. The following year, this question was posed once more as part of a forceful plea to amalgamate game and fisheries initiatives. Accordingly, in 1907, a new Department of Game and Fisheries was formed under the control of a cabinet minister. For the first time, the district game wardens—now seven in number—were expected to exercise their powers exclusively over game *and* fish. Drawn from fishery overseers and deputy wardens, a team of 215 "overseers" was drafted to assist them.

In years to come, wardens would be called overseers and overseers would be called wardens. They were almost one and the same, and both names held sway until 1948 when the term "conservation officer" was introduced.

THE TORONTO DAILY

42ND YEAR — JUNE CIRCULATION, 229,820 — TORONTO, TUESDAY, JULY 17, 1934 — 32 PAGES

NIXON FIRES ALL ONTARIO GA[ME]

ADDS $145,000 TOTAL TO SAVINGS EFFECTED BY HEPBURN CABINET

Ruling Affects 117 Permanent, 500 Deputy Wardens of Department

EXPECT OTHER CUTS

Sweeping Changes at Queen's Park Expected After Cabinet Meets To-day

Fulfilling his promise of a drastic shake-up in the department of game and fisheries, Hon. Harry Nixon to-day decided to discharge every game warden and deputy warden in the province. Their salary is $145,791 per year.

The orders for dismissal have not gone out, but are expected to be in the mails within the next few days, The Star learned.

The sweeping dismissal will affect permanent and temporary game wardens of the districts at London, Ottawa, North Bay, Sault Ste. Marie, Fort William and Sioux Lookout, the seven district headquarters for enforcing the Game and Fisheries Act. Five hundred deputy wardens who receive no salary are also slated to go, it was learned at Queen's Park to-day.

District No. 1 at London has six permanent employees with a

(Continued on Page 2, Col. 2)

TURKEY APOLOGIZES FOR KILLING OFFICER

Ambassador Formally Conveys Regret to British Gov't

London, July 17.—Turkey, through her ambassador to-day, formally expressed her deep regret over the killing of Surgeon-Lieut. J. W. Robinson and the wounding of Lieut. T. A. K. Maunsell, of H.M.S. Devonshire, by Turkish sentries last Saturday.

The officers whose ship was anchored at the Greek island of Samos approached the Turkish coast for a swim and were shot by sentries as they repeatedly failed to heed a challenge.

HOME AND SPORT EDITION

MAYOR WON'T TRY TO BAN MARCHERS SEEING HEPBURN

But Insists Citizens Behind Him in Determination Not to Allow Parade

GUESTS OF CABINET

Never Intended to Prevent Deputation Going to Cabinet, Says Mayor

Mayor Stewart to-day asked that it be made clear, that while he believes he has the citizens behind him in his stand, no attempt will be made to prevent the hunger marchers from calling on Premier Hepburn and his cabinet, but insisted that it be made equally clear that they will be responsible for what may happen.

Premier Hepburn and Attorney-General Roebuck have invited these people to come and see them," said his worship. "No parade or demonstration will be tolerated and Mr. Hepburn and Mr. Roebuck must accept full responsibility for whatever may ensue. Toronto nor its police are not looking for trouble but we desire peace and will maintain it. Be it known that if these people come, they will be guests of Mr.

(Continued on Page 2, Col. 3)

OTTAWA DETERMINED NO TIE-UP IN CANADA

Will Invoke "Peace and Order" Clause of Law, If Necessary

By ROBERT LIPSETT

Ottawa, July 17.—The Canadian government is prepared to exercise every authority vested in it under the "peace, order and good government" clause of the Relief Act, to prevent the industrial upheaval now seething on the Pacific coast of the United States from gaining a foothold in Canada.

The situation in San Francisco, where food is being rationed and milk and bread distributed, "by permission" of the strikers is characterized here as a direct repetition of what happened in Winnipeg in 1919, an attempt to take the administration of law and order out of the hands of properly constituted authorities by force or intimidation.

It is known here that Mr. Bennett had the possibility of present conditions on the Pacific coast in mind when he told parliament that a situation might arise "close to home" which made it expedient to enact the 'peace, order and good government' legislation for another year. The same circumstances were behind lengthier periods of operation for the Pacific coast, between San Francisco and Seattle, is the refusal of Vancouver longshoremen to handle cargoes of United States ships manned by "unfair crews" it is stated here that federal officers are in close touch with the Vancouver situation and the R.C.M.P. officers are unusually alert in watching the movements of known "Communists" in other centres of the Dominion.

CHILDREN OF THE POOR WAIT—AND PRAY

They stand alone in the hidden cities of the poor, desolate and forlorn ... the children of men and women who, jobless, have been obliged to accept the bounty of a generous municipality. No chance have they for picnics to some cool, refreshing island. No hope have they for holidays where they might recuperate from the severe months of winter and years of living on relief. They wait to hear whether there is room enough—and money enough—to go away for 12 days with The Star Fresh Air Fund children. They could share a grand and glorious experience if there was money enough in The Star Fund. Sent your donation yet? Do it now, to 80 King St. W., Toronto.

PARALYZED SINCE BIRTH KIDDIES CAN'T LEAVE HOME

Bodies Twisted and Stiff They Just Gaze at Ugly Ceiling

AWAIT YOUR HELP

In the first house there were two paralytic children—helpless, shivering pathetic—who have never walked in their lives.

In the second house were five children and a mother who hadn't slept a wink last night, tortured with vermin.

In the third house was an Irish mother whose back was tired with fourteen hours of washing clothes for her children.

"It's not an easy life," the woman said. "My husband has been idle these five years. My eldest girl, whose money used to help us going with odds and ends, has trudged the streets daily and can't find work. If it wasn't for a bit of a pension my man gets, we'd be out on the streets. It pays the rent. The welfare office gives us bread and milk . . . and we struggle on like that."

It would have torn your heart to see the two children struck down with paralysis.

They lay with bodies twisted and stiff. Eyes looked straight ahead and had no meaning in them. The

LOVER OF KIDDIES SENDS FUND $1

"I am sorry the amount is not larger, but I am just a working man who loves kiddies," a subscriber writes, sending $1 to The Star Fresh Air Fund.

Dollars are just as welcome as hundred dollar cheques and readers are urged to remember that many mites will help The Star Fresh Air Fund along to a successful conclusion.

Business men are urged to do their part in assisting The Fund. Hundreds of children are anxiously watching the subscription list each day, wondering if enough money will come in to send them away to the country for a holiday.

Mail or bring cheques to 80 King St. W., Toronto. All subscriptions will be acknowledged in The Star columns.

INVITATION TO MAE WEST INCENSES MANY LONDONERS

Also Oppose Bathing Beauty Contest Planned at Port Stanley

"DEGRADING", IS CRY

Special to The Star

London, Ont., July 17.—A wave of opposition to a bathing beauty contest sponsored by the London-owned railway at Port Stanley which attracted increased to-day as critics heard that Mayor George Wenige had invited Mae West, the goddess of romance, to come up and see us" synchronizes rather too closely with the announcement that Miss West's latest motion picture has been banned by leagues of decency, as organiz-

(Continued on Page 2, Col. 3)

SERMON AT FUNERAL IS GIVEN BY SIGNS

Denver, July 17.—Not even the minister's voice will break the silence to-day during the funeral sermon for Billy Toskey, 11.

Billy's parents, Mr. and Mrs. James H. Toskey, cannot speak or hear. So Rev. Hooper E. Chase will give the sermon in the sign language.

The boy died of injuries suffered when he jumped backward from a swing.

T.T.C. PROPERTY PURCHASES OVER $200,000 SINCE 1930

Total Does Not Include Part of Bay St. Terminal Price

FIGURES SUBMITTED

T.T.C.'s city fund purchases with the exception of a piece of terminal properties since 1930 a deputy-controller of the T.C.'s land purchases conducted by Judge J. W. Denton with him to 1934 this year. The expenditures were

NOTED U.S. MASONS VISIT GRAND LODGE

Grand Master of Massachusetts at 79th Communication

M.W. Bro. Curtis Chipman grand master of Massachusetts, and R.W. Bro. R. J. McKechnie, grand marshal of Massachusetts, arrived in Toronto to-day to attend the 79th annual communication of the Grand Lodge of Canada, A.F. and A.M. in the province of Ontario. Other prominent Masons attending the communication include Bro. D. Campbell, grand master of the Grand Lodge of Quebec, and Past Grand Masters W. H. Wardrope of Hamilton, R. B. Dargavel of Toronto and Walter S. Herrington of Napanee, officers. To-day's session of the house of general purposes of the Grand York continued discussing reports from the chairmen of the various standing committees.

Grand lodge will assemble in Central technical school at 10 o'clock to-morrow morning and elect officers for the ensuing year.

Wives and daughters of the assembled Masons are being entertained at the home of Mrs. B. Reed

DRAPER ON PA[RADE] WILLIA[MS]

Provincial C[hief] Stewart Ha[s] tions Ab[out]

PUBLIC M[EETING]

Report Toron[to] To Be Reor[ganized]

Attorney Gen[eral Roebuck] would nec[essarily] film reports [from] police commis[sion] stituted with [J.] Liberal party [had] J. E. L. Starr.

"Will Mr. [Roebuck] the police com[mission] asked Mr. Roeb[uck].

"I have nothin[g] I see there is so the morning pap[er] Will Mr. McF[adden] sidered Mr. Sta[rr wish] ing to comment. plied Mr. Roeb[uck]

Mr. Roebuck [said] ther the argumen[t about] sit. "There is no[t one] is there?" he as[ked] will now have to a[nswer] Mr. Roebuck . . . General Willia[ms] eral Draper n[ot]

(Continued on Page [2])

WAGE WAR AS RESU[LT]

Mass Meetin[g of] ment Worke[rs] Wednes[day]

First shot in t[he] be a wage war in [Toronto] was foreshadow[ed when] ployees of Supe[rior Cloak] on strike after [refusing to] reduction in sa[lary. H.] Kirzner, official [of the] Ladies' Garment [Union]

A mass meetin[g of] ment workers [will be held] to-morrow nig[ht] Lyceum, to [discuss] to Mr. Kirzner, [a gen]eral strike is or[ganized] Toronto such a [comp]letely paralyze at [least] Alleging that [the]

city have vio[lated] Sam Kraisman, pointed out that [the] international un[ion] to organize a[ll] workers, "there [is] with employers [or] by these actions

A 40-hour week rounds of the un[ion] that if this will b[e] on the agenda of put into effect some 400 familie[s] the city relief fu[nd]

An official of t[he] Co. admitted a s[trike] ment.

MRS. PATRIC[K] OVER JU[LY]

Chapter Four: Emergence of the Field Force

At the inception of the Department of Game and Fisheries in 1907, only seven men in Simcoe, Windsor, Belleville, Beaumaris, North Bay, Sault Ste. Marie and Kenora were authorized as protectors of all fish and wildlife. Without uniforms and lacking the support of a unifying governmental strategy, they were neither the ambassadors of conservation nor the resource managers that C.O.s are today. They simply enforced the laws on a part-time basis. These laws, drawn from a newly amended Act, which charted seasons as well as the numbers of fish and game that could be harvested, were based on a Biblical principle. Deuteronomy 22:6 still underlies current law:

If a bird's nest chance to be before thee ... whether they be young ones, or eggs, and the dam sitting upon the young or upon the eggs, thou shalt not take the dam with the young.

The turn-of-the-century wardens were concerned not only with the undue slaughter of wildlife by Ontario's citizens but also with the growing tide of vacationers flowing into the province from south of the border. A report to the Board of Game Commissioners in 1900 told how trains of the Grand Trunk Railway alone had brought 30,000 people

INSET: *Lawrence "Bull" Hemphill (in uniform) was one of the few game wardens who ignored the government decree and continued working. He and a local trapper pose in front of the Department of Game and Fisheries cabin at Missinaibi Lake.*

LEFT: *The headline that disrupted the lives of Ontario's 117 wardens and 500 deputies in July, 1934.*

to the Muskoka Lakes in the course of the previous season.

The goal of many of these travellers was fishing and hunting, and large numbers converged on the earliest hunting camps, which were distributed along the railway tracks between Toronto and Sudbury. Baggage cars would leave the camps laden with deer, thousands of animals being shipped to Toronto's Union Station within a two-week period. Game wardens would ride the trains and make regular checks on the camps.

The wardens' responsibilities grew steadily as the scope of the job widened. In 1914, fur dealers were licensed and, two years later, a $5 trapper's licence was introduced—a direct outcome of the need to protect furbearing animals in the vicinity of logging camps and "other areas where large numbers of men are employed." In a bid to stop illegal trafficking, coupons had to be purchased by trappers intending to trap specific species. These coupons were later attached to traded pelts.

The North American waterfowl population had also been decimated by hunters and the widespread draining of shallow lakes and marshes. To fight this trend, the Migratory Birds Convention was developed in 1916 between Canada and the United States to protect migratory birds. The resulting Migratory Birds Convention Act required the wardens' vigilance, as did the first officially sanctioned wildlife refuges, known as Crown Game Preserves, which, starting in Grey County in 1917, soon extended to the northland.

The government was expecting too much from its tiny field service. It had come as no surprise when the Ontario Game and Fisheries Commission headed by Kelly Evans, reported in 1912 that, while the game and fish laws were adequate, the wardens' organization left much to be desired. Evans called for a complete overhaul of the protective service, as it was dubbed officially, and a permanent force of well-paid officers.

Before any corrective measures could be taken, however, the First World War called many wardens to the trenches of France and Belgium. It was not until 1920 that the complement of field officers was enlarged to

FIGURE 4-1

Trainloads of vacationers from south of the border were lured by the promise of a boundless harvest. The Buckskin Club at Bacon Lake proudly display both flag and harvest.

National Archives of Canada / PA-9008

sixty full-time overseers and seven district superintendents. Henceforth, deputy wardens, rather than pocketing fines levied against offenders, would serve as unpaid volunteers.

In the years that followed the First World War, hunting and fishing accelerated with the proliferation of the automobile. Driven by scarcity, fur prices soared and, in 1924, beaver and otter harvests were cancelled across southern Ontario. A year later, the 7,222 square kilometre Chapleau Crown Game Preserve was set up as a breeding reserve for beaver.

In 1929, the Game and Fisheries Act was amended to empower wardens to search aircraft. One of the concerns was that millionaires might fly into Ontario without licences and carry home illicit game.

The following year, the wardens' growing public profile, the acceleration in tourist traffic and the heavy demands on the field service for game and fish protection led to the formation of a special committee to probe the game-fish situation. The report that followed declared the field service was "far too small" either to check summer tourists adequately or to protect fish and wildlife.

All the aces were held by the lawbreakers, according to the committee. "The offender has all the advantage of seasonal and geographical isolation to carry on his operations," said the report. "He now has good roads and telephones to help him and his fellows. The overseer, on the other hand, is alone, most often in Ontario in the wilderness, is usually dependent purely on his own wits, and yet is practically obliged to catch his man at the moment when engaged in the illegal operation."

An article in the *Toronto Star* on November 17, 1930, underlined the wardens' dilemma, urging that the government "spend a few thousand dollars of the hundred thousand or so they derive from the sale of deer and moose licences for better game law enforcement."

The 1930 special game-fish committee recommended:
- an increase in wardens in northern Ontario;
- uniforms and better equipment;
- an improvement in discipline, training and job qualifications; and
- an end to wardens' reliance on part-time employment.

Although officially full-timers, wardens were so poorly paid that they had little choice but to subsidize their income with extra work. That is, if they could find it. The Great Depression was affecting increasing numbers of people. Poaching violations increased as food was sought by the hungry and the unemployed, and departmental revenue declined as people could not afford to pay for licences. Trafficking in fur, meanwhile, became a popular pastime and professional buyers encouraged settlers throughout the north to trap beaver, especially, in the course of a general closed season.

During the hard times of the Depression, a shocking blow was dealt to

FIGURE 4-2
A rare monster sturgeon snagged from the depths of the Nipigon River. Proud anglers display their prize of two metres weighing sixty-two kilograms—an extra special treat during the Depression years.

Ontario's game wardens. On July 17, 1934, in what became known as the "Hepburn Purge," marching orders were given to 117 wardens and 500 deputies. Also dismissed were all civil servants hired since October, 1933.

Toronto's *Mail and Empire* newspaper commented that the "slaughter" of the civil service through firings "reminds us of the beheadings which took place during the French Revolution."

When the axe fell, convictions for game and fish violations fell too: 810 convictions in 1933 dropped to 491 in 1934—the lowest since records were first kept in 1919. "Within a few days after the game wardens left their posts," declared the *Mail and Empire* of October 16, 1934, "venison was being served to tourists."

Amid the squalor of the Great Depression, the purge created more hardship and exerted a demoralizing effect on the entire Game and Fisheries Department. To this day, there are people in Ontario whose lives were changed irrevocably by the sackings. For example, David Stewart, son of fired warden "Long Dave" Stewart, will never forget that his father's dismissal robbed him of the chance of a university education.

To replace a staff of 117 overseers scattered across the province was a formidable task. For a while, the Ontario Provincial Police stepped in to fill the breach and there was talk of the O.P.P. taking over the wardens' duties for good. There was even a suggestion that every farmer become a deputy warden. Within a short time, however, some of those who were fired were rehired. A few stout characters, such as Parry Sound's Neil MacNaughtan, managed to linger on in spite of being fired. Such was MacNaughtan's reputation that only one member of the local Liberal committee backed the decree from the premier. Even a diehard poacher, who had been twice arrested by MacNaughtan, stepped up to give his support. "He's a perfect gentleman," the poacher told the committee. "He done his job." Lawrence "Bull" Hemphill was another warden who refused to budge. He fired off a telegram to Hepburn exclaiming "Go to Hell!" and kept on working.

Charlie Cook started as a warden on November 1, 1934. Especially glad to be hired because he had lost his telephone company job in the Depression, Cook, now eighty-three years old, will never forget those first lean years on the job. There were no roads then north of the Sault and, in mid-winter, Cook would take the train into the hinterland carrying snowshoes and a packsack containing a piece of canvas, a sleeping bag and several days' supply of food. He would hop off beside a "section house" somewhere along the tracks and snowshoe back for eight to fifteen days checking trappers, logging camps and pulpwood camps along the way. "Times were pretty damn tough," declared Cook, who retired in 1973 a fish and wildlife supervisor at Sault Ste. Marie.

As well as enforcing the growing body of legislation, wardens were getting involved for the first time in other duties. In 1922, the first pheasants were stocked for release to the wild—a job that, once more, called for the overseers' coordinating abilities. In 1928, a fish culture branch was set up. Among its many purposes was the restocking of lakes and the detection of pollution in suspect areas. Overseers became the field link in the operational chain. Their role, in turn, relied heavily on the voluntary efforts of deputy wardens and members of rod and gun clubs. The government was starting to emphasize caretaking in the wardens' job duties. The 1930s and 1940s saw a gradual swing away from protection alone to "wise use" of all renewable resources based on scientific knowledge.

FIGURE 4-3
The first shipment of Hungarian partridges to reach southeastern Ontario was delivered in 1933 into the careful hands of five wardens. They are, from left: Stanley Knapp, Merrickville; Melvin Drew, Sharbot Lake; Irvin Lyons, Belleville; Jack Mundle, Kingston; and Royal Baker, Cornwall.

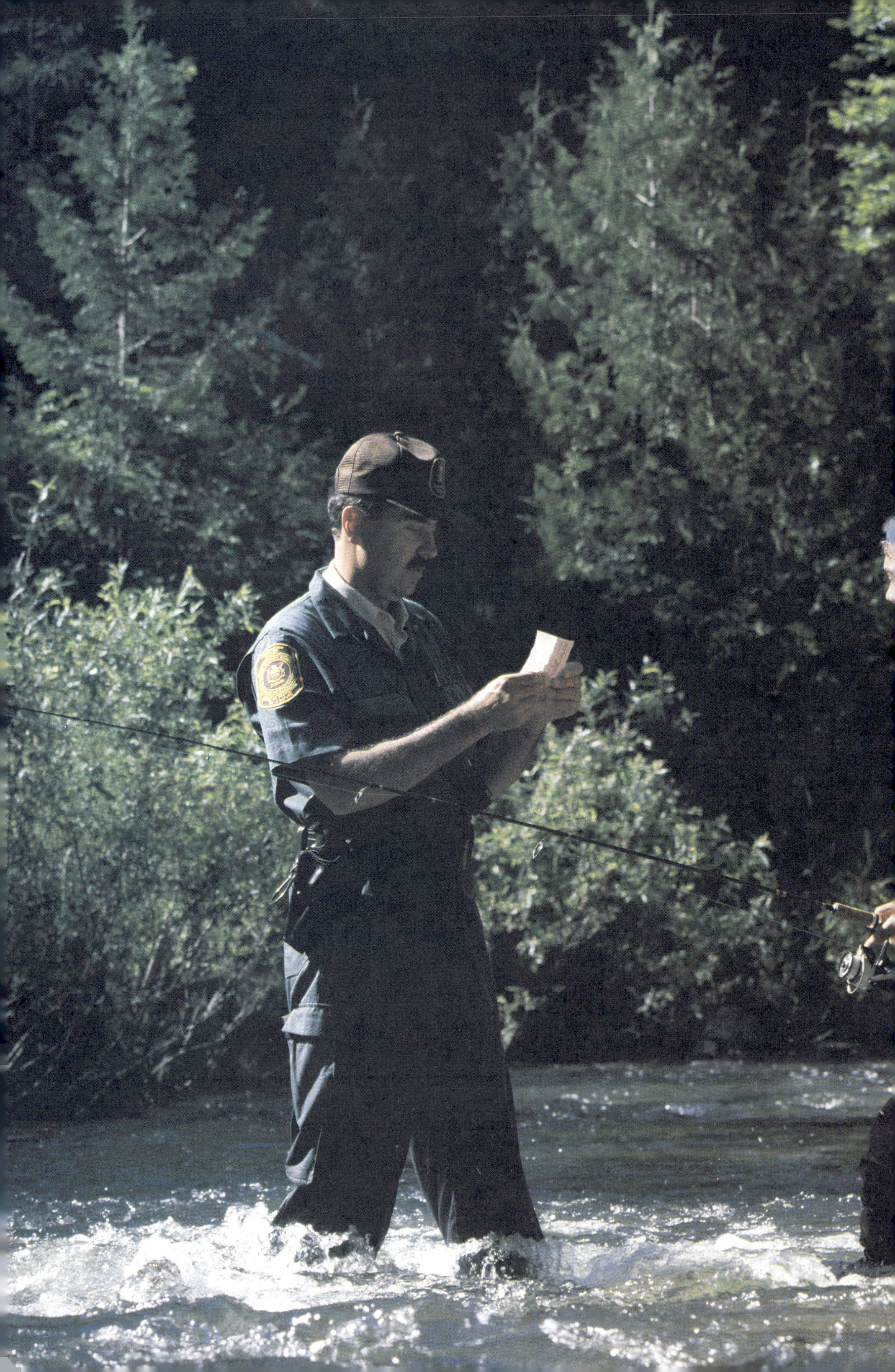

Chapter Five: The Post-War Era

The idea that natural resources could be managed was just beginning to be appreciated in Ontario. Fish culture operations were going full tilt in the mid-1930s and stocking programmes coordinated by field officers distributed millions of fish annually. During 1938, the province of Ontario stocked more fish than all other provinces and the federal government combined.

In the years leading up to the Second World War, deer—absent for decades from southern Ontario's semi-rural areas—returned in droves. A typical newspaper article of the day told of "big herds of deer" roaming the northern half of King township less than forty-eight kilometres from Toronto's city limits. Up until four or five years earlier, said the article, it was a miracle if a lone deer were seen in the township but, recently, as many as thirty-two had been spotted together. Such plenty was directly attributable to the animals' protection under the law.

However, the overall success of a programme based on protective legislation alone was challenged in the 1940s. New questions were being asked that would directly affect the way wardens worked. Had the push for preservation hardened into out-of-date dogma? Could not the ready harvesting of fish and game even contribute to the welfare of the species? Indeed yes, answered an article in Harper's: "Harvesting…is now just as important as protection of breeding stock in maintaining a balance between the game population and its food supply."

Then there was the question of habitat. For the first time, experts were saying that the well-being

LEFT: *All in a day's work. C.O. Mike Evers wades into the Pine River, near Shelburne, to check an angler's licence soon after the opening of the 1991 season. (Re-enactment)*

of fish and wildlife was more dependent on a flourishing habitat than on the length of the hunting and fishing seasons and restrictions on the amount harvested. As the debate intensified, the Second World War broke out and, as in the First World War, many wardens trooped off to the battlefield. When they returned, a new era was dawning—the era of "scientific management."

In 1946, the Department of Game and Fisheries was incorporated into the Department of Lands and Forests and named the Division of Fish and Wildlife. All renewable resources were now under one umbrella. Chief of the fish and wildlife division was Dr. William J.K. Harkness, formerly director of fisheries research at the University of Toronto. Under his leadership, scientific management and public education became the buzz-words of the new regime and conservation shed its static image in favour of a concept that was more flexible and dynamic. Policy was driven by the dictates of biological assessment.

Wardens—supervised by fish and wildlife specialists who reported to district foresters—were directed to spend more and more time on management work in accordance with Dr. Harkness' liberalization of their traditionally tough, protective stance. The transition wasn't always to the wardens' liking.

In 1949, a year after the term "conservation officer" was introduced, the first fur management officers were appointed, mostly from the ranks of overseers. In time, they would become wildlife management officers, providing promotional opportunities for C.O.s.

C.O.s, meanwhile, were encouraged to broaden their outlook, to think provincially rather than just in terms of their own jurisdictions. Jealously guarded patrol areas, where one warden felt obliged to ask the permission of another before venturing beyond his regular stomping ground, were discouraged in a 1946 circular. "The staff have freedom to flow across district or other boundaries where their problems involve inter-district work, such as fires and law enforcement," the circular stated.

The new public conservation values propagated by the department emphasized the thrill rather than the kill: "Limit your take, don't take your limit." This placed a large measure of responsibility on hunters and anglers for the welfare of their respective sports. In sharing the burden, the C.O.s attended new training courses that schooled them in ecological principles as well as offered basic information about the wide range of fish and wildlife species. Said Carl Monk, who started as a conservation officer in 1951: "Such were the demands of the time that the average C.O. could age, sex and tag just about anything that crawled, hopped, flew or ran."

As Jim MacDonald wrote in the *Hamilton Spectator* on January 4, 1968: "To make the most game available to the greatest number of people, [conservation officers] had to know how many hunters shot what. They also had to find out why one species of fish thrived in a certain lake and the other fish didn't. This required a different type of game warden."

This "different type of warden" was also an ambassador of conservation, a public relations person for the welfare of the resource. In 1957, when hunter safety training programs were implemented following increased hunting casualties, C.O.s conducted exams for novice hunters who were compelled to obtain a certificate of competence in gun handling and firearm safety. As in so many ventures, the officer would hold the middle ground, this time between the trainees and the volunteer sports enthusiasts who had assisted with the training. Years later, in 1981, it was made compulsory for all novice trappers to take the fur harvest, fur management and trapping course, and to pass an exam before obtaining a licence.

In post-war years, the basis of fur management became the registered trapline, a tract of Crown land over which the licensed trapper held exclusive rights. By 1950, practically all Crown land was divided according to this system, which adjusted the "take" of fur bearers to the actual production of furs. The object was to encourage trappers to work within biological limits rather than exploit the resources.

In the far north, C.O.s visited each aboriginal community, called all the trappers together and worked from relief maps in recommending boundaries limiting the winter hunting grounds of family groupings within each band area. The officers monitored the trappers and sealed or marked their fur before sale.

C.O.s regularly conducted moose, deer and beaver surveys, ran bag and creel censuses, and stocked lakes with fish and preserves with game. They also live-trapped fur bearers such as fisher, marten, lynx and beaver from game preserves and other well-populated locales in order to restock depleted ranges.

In this role, the C.O.s functioned largely as assistants for the biologists, whose numbers grew within the department from two in 1946 to sixty-seven in 1964. In fact, at least fifty per cent of the wardens' workload now involved implementing management programs in the field or gathering biological data. Even when conducting enforcement roadside checks, officers were expected to glean facts and figures on animals and fish.

On the death of Dr. Harkness in 1960, Dr. C.H.D. Clarke took over as chief of the Fish and Wildlife Branch. Dr. Clarke lived, breathed and wrote about conservation, describing the term as "the wise use of natural resources to provide the greatest good for the greatest number over the longest time."

Yet even as the conservation message was preached loud and clear, C.O.s suffered from a feeling of declining status.

FIGURE 5-1
"Check the breach to make sure the rifle's not loaded," C.O. Bob Trotter instructs a hunter in September, 1961, at Maple. The "show and tell" was part of the department's hunter safety training programme.

Not only did they feel they were treated as work horses for management programmes, but also scant respect or consideration was afforded their enforcement responsibilities. And their wages continued to slide.

When the Game and Fisheries Act was revised into the Game and Fish Act in 1962, the word "constable"—which established in law the C.O.s' ranking as enforcement officers—was cut from the Act. This was a seemingly simple exclusion—but, to the officers, it placed their designation as peace officers in jeopardy. Officer morale suffered further when C.O. badges were issued to many other departmental officials, including foresters, department executives and biologists.

Feeling disparaged, the proud officers soldiered on even as they grew bitter and resentful. Said eighty-one-year-old Wilf Spooner, who was Minister of Lands and Forests from 1957 to 1962: "Conservation officers performed very well considering they weren't a high priority in my organization. Theirs was an area of activity not very well known and not greatly appreciated. Too much was expected of them."

As the apparent regard for conservation officers dwindled, their responsibilities multiplied. To quote from the 1964 annual report of the Department of Lands and Forests, the job of conservation officer "will include" law enforcement, biological surveys of lakes, planting fish, participating in the creel census, evaluating wildlife habitat, assessing deer wintering grounds and measuring degree of browsing, conducting aerial moose surveys and grouse drumming counts, attending meetings of fish and game clubs, operating wildlife check stations, assessing and recommending applications for bait fish and commercial fishing licences, sampling commercial fishing catches, sealing fur, collecting deer and moose jaws for age studies, assigning traplines, issuing trapping licences, providing hunter safety training, visiting schools with a conservation message,

FIGURE 5-2
Trappers and wardens closely cooperate. O.D. Lewis, supervisor at Kapuskasing, tags a beaver pelt owned by Thomas Taylor of the Constance Lake Band at Mamamattawa Reserve in 1955.

reading fish scales to determine their age, report writing "and many other duties." In many areas, C.O.s were also expected to take part in forest fire suppression and conduct provincial land tax assessments of summer cottages, the scaling of saw logs or pulpwood "and other tasks as they are assigned."

The officers' long-standing primary role as enforcers was bound to suffer under this accumulation of duties. And so it did. Over a seven-year period, convictions registered by officers fell from 2,895 in 1956 to 2,045 in 1963—the only time in 100 years that a recurring drop in convictions has been recorded.

In a 1964 report, Frank Walden, supervisor of field services, commented: "It would be pleasant to conclude that at last our public relations program and education program were achieving the desired results." Alas, such a conclusion could not be drawn. Walden cited the "increasing participation by C.O.s in the biological phases of a management program" as one of the main reasons for the decline in enforcement statistics. Since then, a ministry dilemma has persisted: should C.O.s divide their time between enforcing the laws and participating in management work? And if so, how?

Changes came with the launch of the new Ministry of Natural Resources (M.N.R.) in 1972 (which divided the former twenty-two forest districts into eight regions and forty-nine districts), the emergence of the environmental movement and a rise in C.O.s' enforcement responsibilities as lawmakers strove to safeguard nature from a multitude of hazards.

For decades, the C.O.s' legal portfolio had been restricted to the Game and Fish Act, the federal Fisheries Act, the Ontario Fisheries Regulations and the Migratory Birds Convention Act. Starting in the late 1960s, a broadening of C.O.s' legal responsibilities accompanied an urgent public expectation that greater care be extended to the land and waters as well as fish and wildlife. An old rhyme spelled out the massive loophole that was about to be plugged.

FIGURE 5-3
In the glow of his flashlight, C.O. Dino D'Agostini examines a tagged deer carcass at a Spanish River road block in 1949.

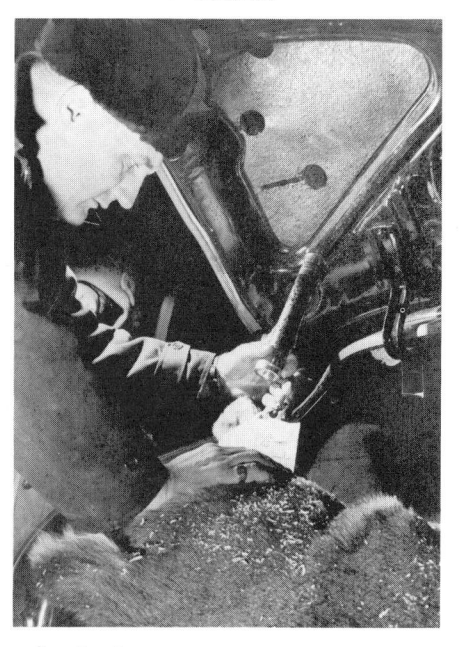

The law is hard on man or woman
Who steals the goose from off the common
But lets the greater sinner loose
Who steals the common from the goose

Henceforth, the drive was on to apprehend the "greater sinner" and the pendulum swung back to a stronger emphasis on enforcement. The base for legal action against despoilers of the environment was broadening. Brought under the C.O.s' jurisdiction was new legislation such as the Canada Wildlife Act, the Endangered Species Act, the Convention in International Trade in Endangered Species of wild flora and fauna

(C.I.T.E.S.), the Petroleum Resources Act and the Wild Rice Harvesting Act. Officers were also largely relied upon to be the "teeth" of such long-standing statutes as the Provincial Parks Act—which empowered C.O.s to act with the authority of police officers within park boundaries—the Public Lands Act, the Beach Protection Act, the Lakes and Rivers Improvements Act and the Export and Import Permits Act.

In 1976, Ralf Aldrich, formerly second-in-command of the R.C.M.P.'s Foreign Service Section in Ottawa, was hired as M.N.R.'s first provincial enforcement specialist, a so-called "super chief" of Ontario's C.O.s. Aldrich spent a lot of time in the districts fostering a much-needed esprit de corps among his staff. Early on, he organized "flying squads" of officers based in various districts who could respond immediately to troubled situations.

In 1980, the Gartley-Dawson report, compiled by regional enforcement specialist Dale Gartley and regional biologist Blair Dawson, called for the continued integration of management and enforcement duties. But the report cautioned: "Management cannot protect the resource without adequate law enforcement." The Ontario Federation of Anglers and Hunters concurred, urging unsuccessfully that the province's complement of officers be doubled to 450.

Successive provincial enforcement specialists felt that pronounced vigilance in the field was the best deterrent against those who plundered or degraded the resource.

Successive provincial enforcement specialists—Ralf Aldrich, Cliff Copeland and Dale Gartley—felt that pronounced vigilance in the field was the best deterrent against those who plundered or degraded the resource. Their impetus, even without a marked increase in officers, saw the number of charges laid annually by C.O.s multiply eight times in thirty years—from 2,318 in 1960 to 17,968 in 1990. Fines leapt dramatically over the same period—from $45,135 to over $1 million.

Several cases investigated in recent years were vast in scope. False entries spotted in the monthly fishing reports of two large tug boats in Lake Huron in 1985 led C.O. Mike Thede to document the largest take of illegal fish in the province's history—over 100,000 kilograms of chub, perch and whitefish.

Ten search warrants were executed in the course of the eighteen-month investigation, which culminated in the laying of seventy charges under the Fisheries Act. A commercial fisher pleaded guilty and in December, 1987, was fined $45,000—the largest fisheries penalty levied in Ontario.

Environmental degradation, especially where water is involved, has commanded officers' attention more than any other single issue in the past decade. In September, 1988, a hydro electric power company started work without a permit on an old dam spanning the picturesque Rocky Saugeen River in Owen Sound District. When the dam's bottom drain gate was removed, thousands of metric tons of silt were sucked from a head pond almost eight kilometres downstream. The water turned chocolate brown and prime spawning grounds of brook trout and brown trout were destroyed.

"It was a pretty sad sight, to say the least," said investigating C.O. Kevin Barber. Thus began Ontario's biggest habitat case, which, in December, 1989, led to fines for the company and its on-site representative of $20,000.

Enforcement is not always a straightforward matter. The relationship between game wardens and aboriginal people over the past century, for instance, has been patchy, fraught with cultural estrangement. Much has been accomplished through cooperative management programmes such as the running of goose camps, cranberry growing projects, and the collecting of deer and moose hides. Nevertheless, "conservation officers have functioned as though the provincial laws superseded treaty obligations that the Crown [had made with aboriginal people regarding] hunting and fishing rights," declared Duke Redbird, past vice-president of the Native Council of Canada.

The water turned chocolate brown and prime spawning grounds of brook trout and brown trout were destroyed.

In February, 1940—after an aboriginal person from Nipissing, who was convicted of poaching, lost his appeal to the Supreme Court of Ontario—the Minister of Game and Fisheries, Harry Nixon, declared that First Nation people must abide by the provincial game and fish laws.

In February, 1991, Minister of Natural Resources Bud Wildman announced that the ministry was modifying its enforcement policy. "We needed to develop an interim policy in order to reflect the guarantee of aboriginal rights in Section 35 of the Constitution and to respond to recent decisions by the Supreme Court of Canada that help define those rights."

"The interim enforcement policy and the legal precedents upon which it is based represent a major shift in philosophy and understanding," said Andy Houser, Director of Compliance Policy Branch. "It recognizes that after conservation objectives are met, aboriginal rights to hunt and fish for personal consumption and social and ceremonial purposes in treaty and traditional areas take precedent over other resource uses. This is hard for many people to accept and makes the job of the conservation officer particularly difficult."

"The difficulty for the C.O.," said Al Stewart, Regional Director in Huntsville, "is that he is walking a fine line....The C.O. must deal with the native who is angry that he is even being checked and the non-native who is angry that the native wasn't charged. The officer ends up having everybody mad at *him*. The officer is caught in the no-man's-land of evolving constitutional rights, Supreme Court of Canada decisions and government policies and attitudes."

But the officers are clearly up to this challenge and are working together with other ministry managers in seeking a new relationship and understanding between non-aboriginal and aboriginal people in Ontario.

C.O.s are also caught up in the conflict between collective rights and the rights of the individual. Said Alan Ryan, a lawyer with M.N.R.'s Legal Services Branch who has prosecuted many officers' cases: "The C.O.s are trying to enforce a system on behalf of everyone. Their defence of collective rights runs headlong into individual rights at a time when individual rights come first, according to the Charter of Rights." More and more, added Ryan, defendants lean on this circumstance by accusing C.O.s of improper or illegal procedures in hope of being acquitted.

Within the ministry's corporate structure, the debate over the division between management and enforcement intensified as the 1980s drew to a close. The Kenrick Report of 1987, pointing out that seventy-five per cent of C.O.s' time was spent on enforcement, urged against the trend towards fully fledged policing, while clearly recognizing the importance of enforcement. But by 1990, officers were, in reality, spending on average eighty-five per cent of their time on enforcement in its broadest sense and many wanted to ensure that enforcement remains a primary function. "The truth is," said retired enforcement specialist Doug Townsend, "that by enforcing the laws, C.O.s *are* managing the resources. Sometimes, the only management we have is enforcement."

In early 1991, a new Compliance Policy Branch was set up within the new Policy Division. Appointed as the first branch director was Andy

> **The Kenrick Report of 1987, pointing out that seventy-five per cent of C.O.s' time was spent on enforcement, urged against the trend towards fully fledged policing, while clearly recognizing the importance of enforcement.**

FIGURE 5-4
Managing resources has always been a concern. C.O.s Jack Catcher (left) and Paul Dreyer measure a plump rainbow trout beside the Credit River in 1974.

Houser, former director of operations for southern Ontario. "The public," said Houser, "expects, in fact demands, that our natural resources and the natural environment receive adequate protection. Whether dealing with fish and wildlife, timber harvest, sand and gravel, petroleum resources or old growth forests, ensuring compliance with the rules is a major part of sound resource management. Conservation officers will play an increasingly important role in achieving compliance and conducting enforcement for all natural resources."

C.O.s are seen as resource ambassadors as well as necessary enforcers by an increasingly conservation-minded public. As people have become more sensitive to environmental issues, the profile of uniformed officers has risen accordingly. The C.O.s' morale has been boosted by a large pay increase in 1990 and constantly upgraded training and equipment. But their numbers are still small. Regional Director Al Stewart said of Ontario's C.O.s: "They have one of the toughest jobs in the organization. All managers have complete sympathy for the situations in which they find themselves."

Certainly, the past 100 years have been a rough and tumble century of hardship and achievement. Conservation officers have, nonetheless, emerged from the fray with pride, confidence and a great deal of respect.

> **As people have become more sensitive to environmental issues, the profile of uniformed officers has risen accordingly.**

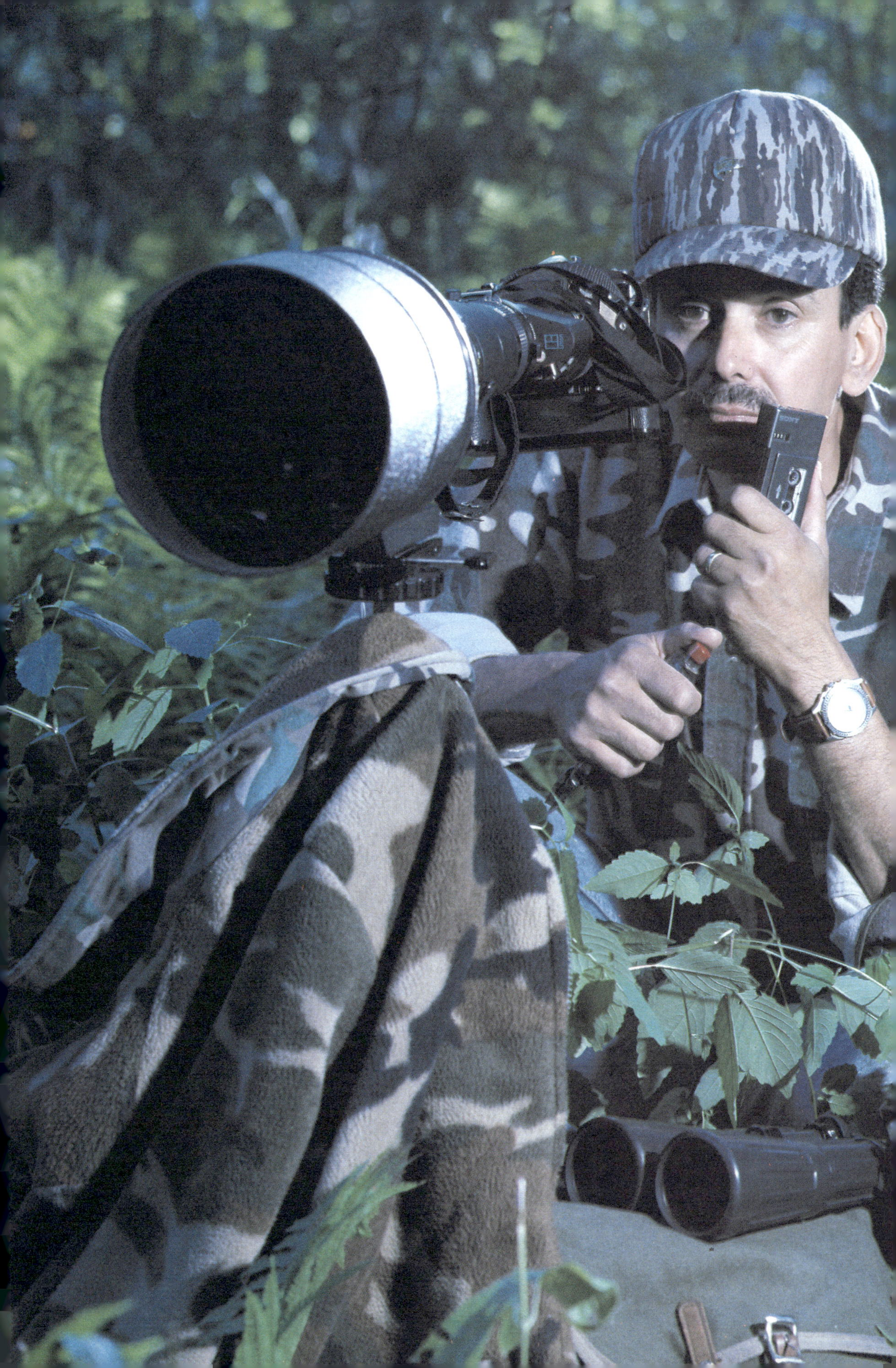

Chapter Six: Give Us the Tools

In the beginning, there was a badge...but that was all. For the first thirty-eight years, there was no Ontario game warden's uniform and overseers at large were expected, quite literally, to provide and paddle their own canoes. They were also required to provide their own firearms, snowshoes, packsacks, axes, knives, camping gear, sleds, dog teams and harnesses. If travel were necessary, which it always was, basic expenses were paid by the government as well as "mileage at the rate of five cents per mile where [the overseer] uses his own horse or boat," to quote from the annual report of the Department of Fisheries for 1905.

The wardens were seemingly long suffering about having to equip themselves with the most elemental tools of their trade. Yet, almost from the start, they clamoured for a steam yacht that would give them a fighting chance against the powerful types of craft used by non-resident hunters and anglers. "I might as well try to stop the sun," lamented Leamington warden Charles Quallins in his annual report for 1893. Besieged by requests from locals for an end to Sunday shooting, he grieved that he had no suitable boat with which to chase and catch offenders. His report continued: "It is no small matter to row fifteen to eighteen miles [twenty-four to twenty-nine kilometres] with a row-boat and then find the hunters gone ...."

INSET: *Night scope image of people and a plane.*
LEFT: *Photo surveillance specialist Ben Attard blends into the scenery as he points his powerful zoom lens (equipped with a night scope) at suspicious activity in the bush.*

Enforcement vigilance was upgraded in 1899 when the steamer *Gilphie* was purchased for $3,250. With a twenty-four-metre hull of white oak, a steel boiler and a top speed of nineteen kilometres an hour, the ship was soon doing "excellent service" on Georgian Bay, its crew managing to destroy a large number of illegal trap nets. By 1905, however, the *Gilphie*—which cost $4,310 a year to run—was considered to have outlived her usefulness. The islands and shores between Penetang and the Bustards, practically uninhabited a few years earlier, were now swarming with tourists and summer visitors and rife with illegal fishing. But shallow waters prevented the *Gilphie* from entering the area and reaching the violators. Meanwhile, another Georgian Bay patrol vessel, the sailboat *Maud*, was leaking badly and needed replacing.

> By 1930, ten motorized patrol vessels were operating in various parts of the province.

By 1930, ten motorized patrol vessels were operating in various parts of the province. But the trusty canoe and rowboat were still the most common form of water transportation for the greater part of the force. Overseer David Stewart—known affectionately as "Long Dave" because he was two metres tall—lived in a log cabin on Herridge Lake near Temagami in the early 1930s and patrolled the lake daily in a green, canvas-covered, department-issued canoe. His son, David Stewart Junior, remembered that for winter patrols Long Dave had a pair of oversized snowshoes made especially by an aboriginal person who lived near Hagar. The snowshoes would be worn over heavy socks, moose hide moccasins and four-buckle overshoes.

"My Dad was a great walker," said Stewart. "One day fire rangers brought him a report about [a group of individuals catching] more than their limit of pickerel, having their picture taken with the catch and then

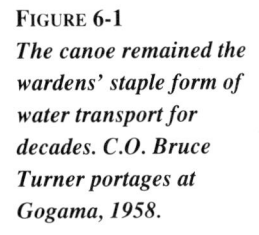

FIGURE 6-1
The canoe remained the wardens' staple form of water transport for decades. C.O. Bruce Turner portages at Gogama, 1958.

throwing the fish into the bush behind their cabin. My father walked nine miles to Jumping Caribou Lake, found the fish, charged the fishermen, and walked back."

Long Dave, who died in 1958 at the age of 84, never wore a uniform and supplied his own .38 revolver and his own axe. That his canoe was provided by the Department made him more fortunate than most. In 1941, warden Alf Hodgson of Lindsay was snubbed by Queen's Park when he requested a canoe to patrol the marshes of the Kawarthas where muskie fishing had become an illegal spring ritual. Deputy Minister D.J. Taylor wrote back: "... in view of the large numbers of young men from your area now serving overseas in the war, there should be an ample supply of canoes from which you could borrow one for the purpose intended."

The Uniform

Until well after the Second World War, the Department had the reputation of being cheap when it came to supplying wardens in the field. One exception related to uniforms. The 1930 report of the special game-fish committee had urged that overseers be both better equipped and in uniform. While decent equipment would be a long time coming, the call for a uniform was answered almost immediately, perhaps because of the strong argument put forward by the committee members. To be without a uniform, said the report, was obviously disadvantageous because a uniform commands respect and is "a warning of organized service." Furthermore, the lack of a uniform could be dangerous "for the reason that lawbreakers generally assume that it is safer to maltreat a citizen than an officer."

Within a few months, most of Ontario's seventy-five wardens were wearing a heavy wool twill tunic with five brass buttons—each bearing a king's crown—and a collar buttoned tightly to the neck. To the delight of overseers who had served in the First World War, the new outfit was a lighter khaki version of the Canadian Army commissioned officers' uniform. To match the outfit, most officers wore Strathcona boots laced up to the knee. In 1933, three years following the first issue, the collar was changed to conventional lapels.

After the Second World War, it was decided that the wardens needed a new look and in February, 1946, a bluish-grey wool tunic was issued. Within a few months, however, the outfit was destined for the scrapheap. The reason: the Departments of Game and Fisheries, and Lands and Forests were to amalgamate.

The following year, after the question of uniforms had been hotly debated, new green whipcord uniforms were issued not only to overseers and fish and wildlife specialists, but also to district foresters, chief rangers,

FIGURE 6-2
Five game wardens model a variety of uniforms while lining up for a photo at Pelee Island during the pheasant hunting season of September, 1938. They are, from left: Bill Flynn, Gordon Buie, Alf Hodgson, Percy Revill and Leslie Bray. "Uniforms were in short supply and officers scraped together what they could from the police and other agencies to make themselves look official," Hodgson recalls.

biologists, timber supervisors, pilots and others, including certain executives at main office. The wardens' uniform was different only in that the tunic had epaulettes and hooks for a Sam Browne belt and holster.

While C.O.s accepted the new uniforms, they objected to the generic nature of the insignia that identified a multi-faceted department rather than an individual charged with the enforcement of the game and fish laws. The fish and wildlife specialists protested the insignia at meetings and through memoranda. But their objections were overruled.

A rather humorous incident involving the uniform hat insignia occurred because of a communications gap in the bureaucracy. While officers of the armed forces, Ontario Provincial Police (O.P.P.), Royal Canadian Mounted Police (R.C.M.P.) and city police forces all swore allegiance to the Queen and replaced their hat badges to reflect the new crown this did not occur in the Department of Lands and Forests. Until 1971, that department continued to supply hat badges carrying the king's crown!

From 1960 to 1965, a different kind of button appeared on C.O.s' green, synthetic parkas—a survival button. If a C.O. was lost in the wilderness without provisions—according to the inventive manufacturer—the parka's six green buttons could be boiled for soup. "I don't ever remember hearing of an officer consuming one of those buttons," said M.N.R.'s Doug Sibley, who has been involved in uniform management for thirty years. "I was always sceptical myself—the buttons certainly looked hard, like plastic."

Shortly after the Department of Lands and Forests became the Ministry of Natural Resources in 1971, the C.O.s' uniform changed again. Replacing the military-style tunic was a green, waist-length Eisenhower jacket. Brown, rather than green, pants were made regulation issue.

In 1989, a new shoulder flash incorporated for the first time a French translation of conservation officer—"agent de protection de la nature." Throughout 1992, to celebrate their centenary, C.O.s are wearing a flash on their left shoulders proudly declaring 100 YEARS.

When overseers became conservation officers in 1948, they were presented with a circular, nickel-plated identification disc. The nondescript disc was not well received by members of the force. In 1953, however, the Department reverted to the traditional shield-type badge, inlaid with sky blue and red enamel. Distributed with a black leather wallet, the badge was an instant morale booster. The badge design, if not the wording, was retained in 1971 with the inception of the Ministry of Natural Resources. But by the summer of 1991, Ontario C.O.s were carrying a new gold, green and blue shield-shaped badge inscribed in French as well as English.

Firearms

Wardens were first offered government firearms soon after the turn of the century. While shotguns, rifles and revolvers were handed out very irregularly—mostly as a result of seizures and subsequent forfeitures—officers usually supplied their own guns until the late 1930s when most officers were issued .32 calibre revolvers as well as handcuffs. During the Second World War, seized weapons were no longer put up for public auction but forwarded, instead, to the war effort "as weapons of protection against sabotage, and other national defence purposes" according to a Department of Game and Fisheries bulletin.

At the time of the merger with the Department of Lands and Forests, some wardens—among them Chapleau's Vince Crichton who carried a 9 mm. Luger from the First World War—were still bearing their own weapons. But the officers' days as armed protectors were brought abruptly to a close in December, 1946, when Dr. William Harkness, the new chief of the fish and wildlife division, ordered the recall of all wardens' firearms in accordance with his new policy of liberalization. He felt that in ten years' time, public education would do away with the need for wardens to enforce the game and fisheries regulations. However, officers were soon reissued revolvers, this time .38 calibre weapons instead of the .32s that had been recalled.

Since then, the .38 calibre handgun has been the C.O.s' standard weapon, but the Smith and Wesson model—originally designed in 1896—was not used exclusively until 1978. In the late 1980s, self-defence batons were made available to C.O.s as an "intermediate deterrent": both side-handle and expandable batons are supplied to officers.

Up until twenty years ago, there were, nonetheless, many C.O.s who resisted carrying a firearm. Preferring to rely on words as a last resort, they either left their holsters at home or filled them with a make-believe weapon such as a hunk of wood or a roll of toilet paper. Some officers felt impeded by the weight of a gun, some believed the sight of a weapon incited troublemakers, and others were uneasy about carrying a firearm they had not received instructions on how to use. But as violence in society has increased, so has the insistence that all C.O.s not only wear their handguns but are able to handle them effectively. In answer to the escalating risks, some officers started to buy their own bullet-proof vests ten years ago. Beginning in 1988, the ministry made available soft body armour, as vests are known, to C.O.s upon request.

Even though C.O.s are instructed to draw their revolvers only when all else fails, they must come to terms with the possibility of shooting someone in a life-or-death situation. Constant training ensures that marksmanship is maintained, but accepting emotionally that one may have to injure, and possibly kill, is another matter altogether.

Said former C.O. Tom Logan, now a justice of the peace in Terrace Bay: "When I was younger, I often wondered: 'Would I shoot a guy if I had to?' My answer was that I thought I wouldn't be able to do it. But you have to come to grips with that question, if not for yourself then for any other C.O. or individual who might be with you. As I got older, I realized that if ever I was confronted with such a life-threatening situation then I could use my revolver."

Kenora C.O. Joan Hubay has reached that decision, of necessity. "A gun is a deterrent and, if they ever took my firearm away, I wouldn't be doing the job," she said.

Transportation Equipment

Transportation equipment has changed dramatically over the years—especially in the last two decades with the introduction of all-terrain vehicles (A.T.V.s) and powerful snowmobiles. As the recreational population has become increasingly mobile, C.O.s have been required to keep pace.

The first motor vehicles—five lightweight Ford trucks—were purchased in 1917 by the Department of Lands, Forests and Mines for forest rangers. Generally, game wardens were not supplied with vehicles until after the last war when blue panel trucks and pick-ups were dispatched to district offices. In the 1930s and 1940s, officers were encouraged to buy their own cars and were paid mileage for patrol work. So satisfying was this arrangement that some wardens objected to the departmental decision to supply officers with transportation. These days, C.O.s are equipped with various green and white vehicles—cruisers, half-ton trucks and four-by-fours—depending on geographical location and the tasks at hand.

Car radios were introduced in the mid-1950s, an innovation that inspired mixed feelings among the enforcers. Said retired C.O. Peter Nunan: "They were a blessing and a curse. You were under closer supervision than ever before. You were no longer free to follow your own hunches. But radios allowed us to do a better job." In the past five years, many C.O.s in southern Ontario have been equipped with car phones.

Red, flashing lights have been standard equipment for C.O.s' cruisers in the modern era. In the early 1970s, the existing red roof and fender flashers were suddenly replaced with yellow lights. "I can vividly remember," said C.O. Pat Brown, "trying to chase people with a revolving yellow light on the patrol car. Few drivers paid any attention—they thought we were tow trucks!" In 1973, an amendment to the Highway Traffic Act made red emergency indicators on C.O.s' vehicles legal for the first time and patrol cars were re-equipped accordingly.

A.T.V.s appeared in the mid-1970s and were put to work at once patrolling back country roads and trails. Three-wheeled A.T.V.s or "trikes" were popular for several years but their stability was questioned after several C.O.s were involved in accidents. A four-wheeler or "quad" is now the authorized ministry A.T.V.

When C.O.s Doug Hyde and Jim Poirier plunged through ice-covered Lake Joseph in March, 1988, their A.T.V.s saved them—they floated! The officers were checking people ice fishing when they fell through a pressure crack leaving them knee-deep in icy water astride their rubber-tired vehicles. Poirier was able to clamber back onto the ice and, holding out his parka, to pull Hyde to safety. "Without those trikes," said Hyde, "it would have been a different story."

Since the days of the steamer *Gilphie* on Georgian Bay, more and more boats have been used by C.O.s. In the late 1940s, officers Dino D'Agostini and Harold Silva patrolled Georgian Bay in an eleven-metre mahoghany patrol boat that had been used for search-and-rescue by the Royal Canadian Air Force during the Second World War. With its graceful lines and 195 horsepower Buchanan engines, the boat had plenty of power and finesse. "But she wasn't that good for our purposes," said D'Agostini. "She wasn't the type of boat you could use for checking fishermen."

Today, there are patrol boats of all shapes and sizes on great and small lakes and rivers—from former commercial fishing vessels to Boston whalers, from freighter canoes to propeller-driven airboats and outboards. Between 1980 and 1991, Napanee District C.O.s cruised Lake Ontario in one of the larger patrol vessels of modern times, the *Percina*, which

FIGURE 6-3
Queen of the North Channel, the mahogany patrol boat Sylva *regularly carried officers Dino D'Agostini and Harold Silva around Georgian Bay in the late 1940s.*

"Policing" On Skates

FIGURE 6-4
Self-equipped for Lake Erie's deep freeze, C.O. Roy Muma skated forty kilometres a day to check on the ice fishing during the winter of 1941.

measured nine-and-a-half metres and required a crew of three officers. In the end the *Percina*'s size was the overriding factor in the decision to trade down to a smaller vessel, the six-metre *Mederios*. "With the expanding charter boat fishery," said Garry Himburg, fish and wildlife supervisor, "we needed a boat that is easier to handle and can be put on a trailer."

Snowmobiles have proliferated since 1947, when the original Bombardier—looking like a small aeroplane—was first seen patrolling Lake Simcoe. Jack Ellis, son of Simcoe overseer Sandy Ellis, remembered his father and other officers using a Bombardier to swoop in on unsuspecting people ice fishing. The machine, which uttered "a terrific roar," travelled at an incredible speed.

"Back then," wrote Ellis Jr., "a few 'sports' used to prefer to spear lake trout rather than catch them on a line legally. Some of these fellows had cut holes in the roofs of their fish huts to accommodate an extra-long spear handle and would bait the hole to entice the trout within spearing range. The officers would scan the fish huts with binoculars, looking for a protruding spear handle. With the Bombardier they could close in so fast that they were able to catch the poachers red-handed before they could ditch the evidence."

Some wardens, however, were still wearing snowshoes when poachers were equipping themselves with snowmobiles—a most uneven match. In an open letter to fellow members of the Peterborough Fish and Game Association in 1968, president Bob Record painted a pathetic picture of snowshoe-wearing local C.O. Johnny McCulloch trying vainly to chase deer hunters as they roared past him on snowmobiles.

"It is a well-known fact that the poachers in our area are using the finest equipment that money can buy," Record's letter declared. "They have two-way radios, snowmobiles and insulated suits as well as jack lights and guns." Whether or not the open letter had any direct effect, within forty-eight hours of Record's comments being reported in the media, McCulloch was riding a brand new snow machine, courtesy of the department!

Before wardens laid eyes on the earliest snow machines, overseer Roy Muma relied on some equipment of his own to police the frozen shoreline of Lake Erie—a pair of skates! In February, 1941, he covered forty kilometres a day skating among the hundreds of people ice fishing, mainly non-residents, populating an area up to five kilometres offshore between Erie Beach and Port Colborne. Muma's mission was to make sure non-resident ice-cutters were in possession of provincial licences. The officer on skates attracted much attention from the media, with the *Niagara Falls Review* enthusing on February 18, 1941: "Game warden Roy Muma of Chippawa is probably one of the most energetic custodians of the game life of the province that can be found anywhere in Ontario."

As soon as the Ontario Provincial Air Service (O.P.A.S.) took wing in

1924 with an initial fleet of thirteen aircraft, overseers' mobility was greatly enhanced by the "nervous system of the north," as the O.P.A.S. was regarded. In 1931, Frank MacDougall was appointed the first flying superintendent of Algonquin Park. He would inspire fear and dread in poachers' hearts by scanning his domain at a low altitude from the open cockpit of his Fairchild KR-34 biplane.

After the war, various aircraft were used increasingly for management projects, primarily for stocking lakes and rivers with fish and for conducting surveys of moose, deer and beaver. In the far-flung Moosonee District—which comprises twenty-two per cent of Ontario's land mass—more exotic aerial surveys have been conducted to count polar bears, Beluga whales, walrus and caribou.

Former Parry Sound officer John Macfie was involved in the aerial moose census for twenty-five consecutive winters. "We would find their trails first and then orbit tightly at somewhere between 400 and 800 feet [120 to 240 metres] to spook them out of the evergreens," he said. "A lot of northern C.O.s spent a lot of their winters gazing down into the trees and throwing up."

Macfie told of an outstanding pilot, George Campbell, who had a disconcerting tendency to doze while flying a Beaver for long distances. "We might fly transects of a hundred miles [160 kilometres] or so, counting beaver houses," Macfie went on. "The job of the pilot was to fly straight and level. But George had a habit of going to sleep and would only wake up when the

After the war, various aircraft were used increasingly for management projects, primarily for stocking lakes and rivers with fish and for conducting surveys of moose, deer and beaver.

FIGURE 6-5
Snowshoes were invaluable in the good old days. C.O. John Macfie (centre) is pictured inspecting a trapline near Bearskin Lake in the farthest reaches of northwestern Ontario in January, 1951. He is accompanied by Elizier Beardy (left) and Tommy Fiddler.

plane started to bank. Still, George was a better pilot than most even when half asleep, and the best of any I flew with at locating moose."

In the early 1970s, the job of flying enforcement officer was created after the ministry was urged to take action against illegal flying activity and illegal hunting in northern Ontario. Accompanied by a pilot, C.O. Bob McGillivray operated out of Thunder Bay for three years followed by Lorne Hudson, who was based at Dryden, and finally Gord Pollock, from 1980 to 1984.

Lorne Hudson, inter-regional enforcement officer from 1974 to 1980, investigated charter services and aerial hunting, seizing planes as well as guns and game. He often conducted undercover investigations to reach the source of illicit activity. But swooping down to make arrests—usually in a two-seater 150 horsepower Super Cub P18A, designed for crop dusting—had its difficulties. "I had to quit seizing firearms because the plane would get so overcrowded that we could hardly take off," said Hudson. "I once seized thirty-five rifles and shotguns weighing ten to twelve pounds [five to six kilograms] each and we didn't have any room left in the plane."

Helicopters have been used extensively by C.O.s both for management and enforcement work. They can be more than useful as Peter Nunan learned when conducting an aerial patrol over the Ontario-Minnesota border in the fall of 1968. Below lay a narrow river bounded on one side by the United States and on the other by Canada. Below, also, were two hunters. One was in a canoe on the river and the other was walking along the Canadian bank.

"When they saw us," said Nunan, "the man in the canoe started paddling furiously for the American side while his friend was shaking his fist at him. The pilot said to me: 'Do you want that fella?' When I told him I did, he swung low over the river and the blades of the chopper blew the canoe back to the Canadian side." After Nunan had landed nearby, the canoeist's companion, angry at being deserted, confided: "I'm so glad you got him back." Both men were subsequently charged and convicted for hunting without a licence.

Technological Aids

Besides benefitting from advanced transportation on land, water, ice and in the air, C.O.s are equipped with a wide range of technological aids to enforcement. The growth in hardware over the past ten years has been staggering.

Highly sophisticated moose, deer and bear decoys have been the ruin of many an illegal hunter. Sometimes, mounted roadkills are used. On other occasions, the decoys—often rendered particularly enticing by reflective

FIGURE 6-6
C.O. Al Pozzo unloads beaver pelts from an aircraft at Wawa in March, 1961.

eyes—are fashioned out of styrofoam or from plywood covered with burlap. Hunters are inclined to react with startled embarrassment when arrested for pumping bullets into larger-than-life dummy animals.

Word travels fast, however, and hunters became wary of decoys after a rash of arrests in the 1989 hunting season. That's when Rainy River C.O. Kevin Elliott set to work to "change the rules" by designing a remote-control decoy with a moving head. Just before the 1990 season opened, he mounted the hide-on-wood decoy in a small, overgrown field on a quiet highway north of Stratton. Some ninety minutes later, a man with a rifle pulled up in a car and stared. Elliott takes up the story:

"About fifteen seconds into this viewing opportunity, I turned the head in his direction and was met with an instant KER-BANG!, then another and another. In fact, he didn't stop shooting until he turned and saw me seated beside him in his car. His first words, not counting profanity, were: 'That's not a decoy, is it?' and when I said 'Yes' he replied: 'But it moved!' For a few minutes I thought I had him convinced that it was all a figment of his imagination, but he didn't buy it." The swivel-headed decoy deer's first day of work netted four convictions, $5,800 in fines, two rifles and seven years of hunting suspensions.

In the old days, C.O.s always had to be on the scene in person to detect violations. These days, there are alternatives. On many occasions, electronic homing devices planted in the hides of illegally slaughtered animals have led officers to the perpetrators of a crime. Live and remote surveillance photography—using cameras mounted in a tree, for example, or in a parked vehicle—can record vital information on habitat destruction or illegal sale of wildlife.

Powerful lenses can zoom in on suspects trading in endangered species and can even record the numbers of bank notes changing hands on the far side of a parking lot. Surveillance photography does not rely upon daylight; night scopes on video and still cameras and binoculars magically magnify existing light 50,000 times.

In September, 1987, C.O. Ben Attard, photographic specialist with the Special Investigations Unit, conducted a stake-out of several days' duration in the bush near Kenora before shooting all-important pictures of hunters unloading an illegally slaughtered moose from an aircraft. "Photography is an exacting science and a picture is truly worth a thousand

FIGURE 6-7
C.O. Doug Marshall carries a deer decoy to its appointed position in the bush near Port Carling in 1991.

words in court," said Attard. "Working night and day on different projects we never know what to expect and must be ready for anything."

Radio scanners are used to intercept C.B. radio messages that may reveal clues to illegal activity, and officers conducting delicate undercover work are often equipped with electronic "body packs" to maintain contact with back-up teams positioned nearby. If anything goes wrong, the support group knows immediately and can provide swift assistance.

The wonders of forensic science have been harnessed to aid many investigations since the mid-1950s. In one of the first cases involving ballistics experts, C.O. Dino D'Agostini was able to show in 1954 that cartridges recovered near two dead moose had been fired from a hunter's .303 Lee Enfield rifle. The hunter claimed in a Sudbury court that he had been charged by the animals and had fired in self-defence—but R.C.M.P. ballistics testimony showed the bullets had entered *behind* the shoulders. The hunter was fined $300 for killing a bull and cow moose two weeks before the season opened.

In Sudbury in March, 1991, a court accepted in a poaching trial—for the first time in North America—the validity of the identification method known as D.N.A. fingerprinting. Conservation officers were able to show that blood on a bag found on an island where hunting was not permitted came from deer that three Killarney men were found unloading from their boat a day later. The men claimed the deer had been shot in an area where hunting was allowed.

FIGURE 6-8
The eyes tell the story. Deluged with paperwork during Operation Falcon, C.O. Ron Jean-Marie craves deliverance from mountains of files.

The identification was made by comparing patterns in the deer's D.N.A.—the chemical blueprint that stores every living being's genetic code—to the D.N.A. in the blood on the bag. "We looked at fifteen unrelated deer and found a perfect match of [D.N.A.] fingerprints only between the blood in the bag and the hunters' deer," said Bradley White, a McMaster University biologist who analysed the samples.

As well-equipped as Ontario's C.O.s may be, they yearn for a technological reprieve from the job that, traditionally, has the least appeal: paperwork. Whereas the early wardens contented themselves with a diary to record, in brief, their daily activities, contemporary officers fill out activity reports that account for every hour of every working day, detailing locations visited, warnings given, charges laid, contacts made and more.

In Moosonee District, where ninety per cent of the population speaks Cree, paperwork embraces the frequent use of manual typewriters fitted with Cree "syllabics" or lettering. Local interpreters are brought in to translate C.O.s' management and enforcement information bulletins for the benefit of First Nations scattered across the district's 221,000 square kilometres. Now that software in syllabics has been developed, the hope is that software for Cree will soon follow.

Certainly, word processors are being used increasingly across the province, but there is no end in sight to paper necessities such as federal and provincial summonses and information, offence and prosecution reports, caution cards, young offenders' forms, daily activity reports, diaries, notebooks, seizure tags and receipt books for seized items. These pen-pushing items may not be exciting, but they are a critical part of law enforcement. They satisfy the demands of documentation and evidence gathering as well as a thirst for statistical information.

Income

This discussion of tools has so far left out one important item: wardens' salaries. Perhaps no change in circumstances over the years has been more striking than the overwhelming improvement in pay. The initial pittance of $10 a month offered part-timers in 1892 rose steadily, but not excessively. The Ontario Game and Fisheries Commission report of 1912 spoke of overseers being paid "such trifling sums for their services that they are forced to busy themselves in other occupations in order to earn a living and consequently have but little incentive to respect the dignity of their position or to discharge their duties energetically."

By 1939, the starting salary was $93.75 a month, a sum indelibly impressed upon the memory of those Game and Fisheries overseers, who had struggled through the Depression years in various jobs. Some of them joined the department in order to eat. However, any meals consumed while on duty and away from home had to be, well, moderate to say the least. Jean Farewell, of Toronto, who checked overseers' expense accounts at Queen's Park during the 1930s, was instructed to watch for the slightest extravagance. "If they were spending more than seventy-five cents for a meal we'd have to check up on them," she said.

By 1951, the wardens' monthly wage had leapt to $166—$10 a month more than the O.P.P. But by 1964, C.O.s were being paid a starting salary of $267 a month, whereas by comparison, in the ten year span between 1959 and 1969, an entry-level department biologist's salary increased from $367 to $623 per month. "The job was very poorly paid," recalled retired C.O. Harry Gingrich. "You couldn't live on it."

In 1970, C.O.s' pride and dignity were dealt a blow. C.O.s were "broad-banded" in the third category of resource technicians series. Disliking this RT3 classification, C.O.s were soon referring to the broad-banding as "a theft of recognition." Of sixty-four fish and wildlife enforcement agencies in North America, only Ontario and Nova Scotia placed their officers in this category.

Bitterness spread through the ranks. In 1979, the Ontario Conservation Officer's Association was formed and for the next six years lobbied unsuccessfully for reclassification. In May, 1985, 199 C.O.s out of 235 filed grievances claiming that their primary enforcement role was being ignored. It took time and much negotiating, but in April, 1990, it was announced that Ontario's C.O.s had won a twenty-four-and-a-half per cent increase that brought the top salary to $45,500 a year and reclassification.

The new pay package made Ontario's C.O.s the third highest paid wildlife enforcement agency in North America after the Yukon and the U.S. Fish and Wildlife Service.

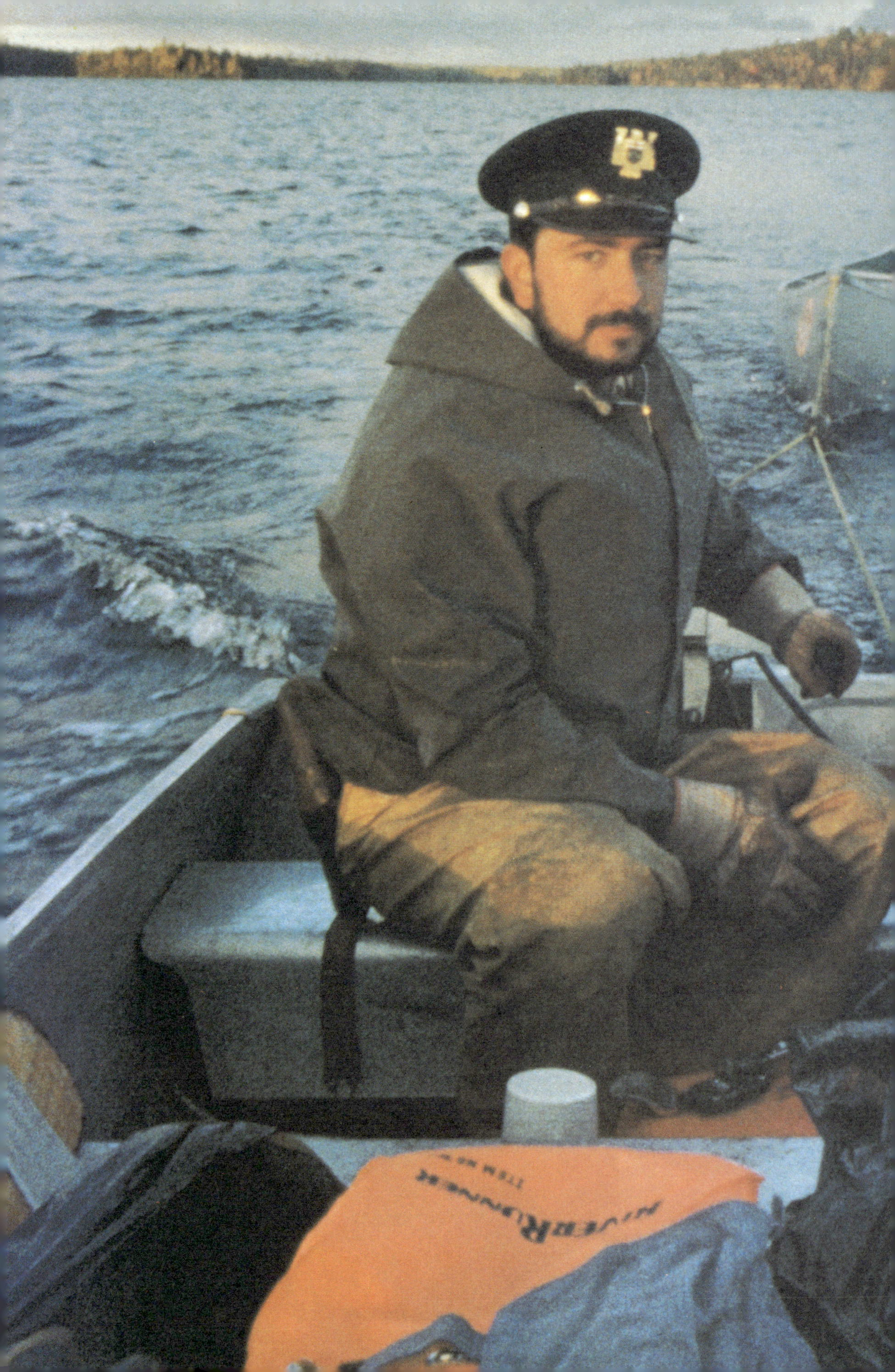
RIVERRUNNER

Chapter Seven: Running the Gauntlet

A conservation officer's every working day is fraught with the prospect of danger. Whether the threat comes from hostile terrain or an aggressive human being, the C.O. is expected to meet the challenge with steady nerves and sound judgement. Statistics and wardens' reports concerning the manner in which some officers have been injured and killed answering the call of duty show clearly that the will and ability to run the gauntlet is indispensable. The warden's job is hazardous indeed.

In 1984, the Audubon Society of the United States advised that the chances of a conservation officer being killed on duty were nine times greater than those of a police officer. Statistics for 1987 revealed that fourteen per cent of Ontario C.O.s— or one in every eight members of the force—were assaulted on the job. Studies have shown that roughly sixty-five per cent of people facing serious charges laid by C.O.s in Ontario have criminal records.

Time and time again, C.O.s who are often alone must face groups of hunters and anglers in wilderness locations after dark. Often, these people are armed and, when confronted, may be ill-tempered, unpredictable and prone to violence, particularly if intoxicated. Furthermore, the high penalties for wildlife infractions tend to instill a stubborn resistance—a fight or flight response—from those who are caught breaking the law.

The task of enforcement in the bush accounts for only some of the physical risks, however. Officers are liable to be called upon to quell rowdyism in provincial parks, to investigate organized crime, to

LEFT: *C.O. Rick Stankiewicz faces the hazards of a lonely patrol.*

FIGURE 7-1
It's twilight on Manitoulin Island as C.O. Ian Anderson approaches a suspect. "It's an absolute reality that conservation officers are going to be faced with dangerous situations," declared Anderson, past president of the O.C.O.A.

conduct search-and-rescue missions and even to settle domestic disputes.

"It's an absolute reality that conservation officers are going to be faced with dangerous situations," declared Ian Anderson, past-president of the Ontario Conservation Officer's Association. "As an association, officer safety is one of our primary concerns." He speaks from personal experience. Although standing 1.93 metres and weighing ninety-eight kilograms, Anderson has been choked, kicked, bitten and threatened with loaded firearms in the course of his career.

Violence has always been an occupational hazard in populous as well as remote areas. As long ago as 1912, a report of the Ontario Game and Fisheries Commission mentioned with some alarm that "even within the sound of the bells of the City Hall of Toronto" shots were fired at an officer who was attempting to stop illegal fishing in Toronto Bay.

Practically every veteran C.O. has personal stories detailing harrowing escapades, narrow scrapes, chases, physical battles, threatenings and shootings. Provincial enforcement specialist Dale Gartley, while admitting he was an "aggressive" officer in his time, has been assaulted several times while on patrol. Over a few weeks one spring, while he was investigating fish poaching activity in the Thames River area, shots were fired at Gartley on several separate occasions.

Since 1972, four Quebec C.O.s have been killed on duty, the latest being Luc Guindon who was shot with a crossbow by a moose hunter in the woods ninety kilometres north of Montreal in 1989. The Quebec Conservation Officers Union told the ensuing inquest that the dangers of the job have increased slowly but surely over the last twenty years to unsettling levels with "more and more violent situations."

It is surely remarkable, then, that while several Ontario C.O.s have died on duty in hazardous circumstances, not one C.O. has been murdered in the past 100 years—officially, that is. A closer look reveals that the deaths of two wardens are highly suspicious but no one will ever know beyond all reasonable doubt whether a killer or killers can be blamed.

The first of these "murder mysteries" involves an officer by the name of John Billings, a First World War hero who was awarded the Distinguished Conduct Medal for "conspicuous gallantry and devotion to duty in the field." Forty-two-years-old, well-liked and experienced, Billings was last seen alive on January 8, 1926, when he left home with a local guide, Joe Stringer, to investigate illegal trapping along the southern boundary of Algonquin Park. When the two men had failed to return after a week, a search party set off in pursuit and eventually made a grisly discovery.

At twilight, the charred remains of Billings and Stringer were found in the cold ashes of a lumber company cabin near Whitney. It appeared that the men—who were identified by durable articles from their pockets—had been shot and covered with piles of hay and wood before the cabin was set ablaze. An empty rifle cartridge was found nearby. The shell had apparently been fired recently and did not fit Billings' gun. Many footprints were found in the snow around the cabin door and one man's tracks led away from the scene—presumably those of the murderer. Medical authorities later declared that the fire must have been fed continuously in order to maintain sufficient heat to char the victims' bones.

Provincial Constable S.J. Elliott secured a warrant for the arrest of a twenty-four-year-old trapper he believed had done the deed. The accused maintained at the inquest that he had been tracking a fisher in northern Haliburton County at the time. He even produced two fisher pelts to prove that his hunting had been successful.

Enough doubt was cast on the Crown's case for the trapper to be set free after the hearing. Presumably, Billings and Stringer had died as a direct result of a monstrous crime. But no one could say for sure and, to quote the *Pembroke Standard*, the tragedy was to "go down in history as one of the many unsolved mysteries of the woods."

Wilf Faubert, also a forty-two-year-old veteran, was another warden whose death generated suspicions. In March, 1945, Faubert was run over by a train on the Canadian National tracks east of Minaki. "What happened is anybody's guess," said his son, Roy Faubert, who heard the news in Calgary where he was training to be a pilot. "All I know is that he liked his job and that he was serious about protecting the environment and wildlife." Based at Minaki—his sixth northerly posting in an eighteen-year career—Faubert always wore a tie on duty and travelled a lot by train. His death poses many unanswered questions.

"The suspicion was," said Charlie Bibby, former fish and wildlife supervisor for Sudbury District, "that Faubert was getting too close to operators in the illicit fur trade, that he was murdered and his body laid on the tracks so that people would think he had killed himself." Again, proof was an elusive commodity and no one was apprehended.

Warden George Mortimer ("Mort") Parks had a nasty brush with death in the 1920s when he was travelling by horse and buggy from North Bay to Mattawa. As he rounded a curve in the road, someone shot the reins out of his hands and his horses fled, eventually wrecking the buggy. Parks—who served from 1908 to 1947, most of the time as supervisor for the northeastern part of the province—never did determine who did the shooting, but said he had his suspicions.

FIGURE 7-2
Warden John Billings (right) receives his Distinguished Conduct Medal for bravery from H.R.H. the Prince of Wales (later King Edward VIII) on Parliament Hill in 1919. Seven years later, Billings was found dead in mysterious circumstances near Algonquin Park.

Many death threats have been made against wardens over the century, but perhaps no C.O. other than Dave Kenney has been spectator to a murder plot against his own person.

Back in 1978, Kenney stumbled upon a network of gun thieves when he visited a local dealer in hopes of adding to his antique firearms collection. Instead of antique guns, Kenney was shown a selection of powerful restricted weapons—including a fully automatic machine gun. Troubled by what he had seen, he tipped off the O.P.P.

The thieves learned of Kenney's tip and reacted by hatching a scheme to kill him, a scheme detected by an undercover police officer who had infiltrated their ranks. Their plan was to shoot a partridge out of season, trail Kenney from Espanola District Office, then stop his vehicle and shoot him. The out-of-season partridge was to be left at the scene with the intent of misleading investigators.

On the day Kenney's murder was to be committed, an O.P.P. helicopter followed the pair of would-be assassins as they drove along Highway 17 from Sudbury towards Espanola. The men were arrested at gunpoint at a police roadblock and later sentenced to six years in jail for conspiring to commit murder. In the "sting" operation precipitated by Kenney's tip-off, gun shops were raided across Canada and more arrests were made.

To illustrate the hardships C.O.s must face, a 1948 edition of *Sylva*—a magazine published by the Department of Lands and Forests—included a blow-by-blow account of an arrest made in the wild by C.O. Nelson Jones.

The story starts with Jones and a local trapper following tracks leading into Algonquin Park on the morning of November 30, 1947. Blood on the snow beside a beaver house informed the pair that a beaver had been taken illegally. Nearby was a shelter containing a sleeping bag, wool blankets, a considerable supply of food and traps and two beaver pelts. Jones sat waiting in the shelter until he was alerted by the sound of someone breaking wood. He takes up the story:

"I saw a man approaching carrying an armful of wood, an axe and a bag of traps, also a gun slung from a shoulder strap. As he came nearer, I saw he was quite large in stature with a heavy growth of whiskers. I walked out a few feet to meet him and spoke. Until this time, he had not noticed me. Stopping abruptly, and before I had time to speak again, he asked me with a frown, 'Are you a game warden?'

"I replied that I was and showed him my credentials. As I did this, I informed him he was under arrest and that he would have to go out with me. I asked to see the gun he was carrying. At this he said, 'You stay back 'fore you get hurt. You see no gun.' He threw the wood and bag of traps on the ground. I then told him it would be better to talk to me and not try getting rough. He then said, 'I'm a big man and I've seen bigger men than you. You couldn't handle me,' and added, 'I'm going now, but not with you.'

"At this, he started to run towards the beaver lake. Running about twenty-five or thirty feet [eight to nine metres] on the snow-covered ice, I caught up to him, grabbing him by the left shoulder. He wheeled and shoved the rifle, which later proved to be a 44-40 Winchester, in my stomach. I pulled the blackjack from my pocket and struck the gun, knocking it to one side. He said, 'Be careful, this gun is loaded,' and began to run again.

"After another sprint, I caught up and as I did, he swung the gun as a club, striking me on the right side, breaking the sixth and eighth ribs. He ran on and, when in the centre of the lake, as I was again almost upon him, he swung with the gun again, striking me on the nose and causing it to bleed. With another swing he caught me across the left shoulder and the back of the left hand, as I attempted to protect my body from the blow. He again ran on and, by this time, we had almost crossed the lake.

"He started up the bank into the bush with me right behind him and I struck at his arm holding the gun. As I swung, he lowered his head in an attempt to knock me down off the bank. The blackjack struck him a hard blow on the head, inflicting a wound which bled freely. This, however, did not slow him down. He ran towards a large jack pine. I came around the tree and he swung the axe, which buried itself in the tree as I jumped back.

"By this time, I was in a state of anger and more determined than ever that he was not going to get away. As he ran around another tree some yards on, I closed in on him before he had a chance to swing again. Seizing him by the arm, I used a judo hold, throwing him to the ground and on his back. He fell heavily and the rifle flew up, striking him over the left eye, causing a laceration which allowed blood to drain into his eye. I held him on his back in the snow…"

Jones told how he picked up the man's axe and gun and made him walk ahead to the shelter where, in gentlemanly fashion, he built a fire, boiled some water for tea, bathed and bandaged the man's head and gave him some sandwiches. A thirteen-kilometre hike to the warden's car followed, then a journey of eighty-two kilometres to the district office at Pembroke. At a subsequent court hearing, the prisoner was convicted of resisting arrest, pointing a firearm, carrying a firearm in the park, hunting in the park, killing two beavers in closed season and destroying beaver houses. His punishment: a sentence of eight months in Guelph Reformatory.

Aside from human violence, harsh experience has shown that the greatest perils facing officers in the wild are water, ice, wind and human frailty.

Lee Branscombe had only been a C.O. for about two years when he set out with deputy warden Jim Noble in a motor-powered skiff to cross Collins Inlet channel, near Killarney, on a windy November evening in

> **"After another sprint, I caught up and as I did, he swung the gun as a club, striking me on the right side, breaking the sixth and eighth ribs."**

1955. The officers were planning to check deer hunters at a camp beyond the commonly choppy waters of the channel. Hours later, the empty skiff was washed up on shore and a search began for the missing men.

Although the waters of the channel were dragged for several days, the effort recovered only a lever from Noble's rifle and a boot belonging to Branscombe. The wardens were swept out into Georgian Bay, or so it is surmised. Their bodies were never found.

> The wardens were swept out into Georgian Bay, or so it is surmised. Their bodies were never found.

In more placid and murkier waters, C.O.s Bob Guenther and Carl Liddle died in October, 1965, while patrolling the vast expanse of Luther Marsh, a duck hunters' paradise lying between the communities of Arthur and Orangeville. Throughout the waterfowl season, officers were stationed in the marsh in five-day shifts. They patrolled on foot, in cars and in a green propeller-driven airboat.

Guenther and Liddle, a younger officer who was unable to swim, were on duty in the airboat on the day they died. The first indication of a serious mishap came with the sighting of the boat, abandoned and drifting near the shore, the propeller broken. The authorities were notified and a search was initiated.

Retired Cambridge C.O. Harry Gingrich remembered receiving a distress call late that evening. Starting that night, and for the next three days, he drove, trekked and paddled across the marsh, hailing the men through a megaphone and shining his car headlights over the water. On the fourth day of the search—conducted by 200 men, many boats and several aircraft—skin divers recovered a hip wader and a Lands and Forests' parka. The following day, the officers' bodies were found three metres apart in two metres of water. Liddle's body was fully clothed while Guenther had apparently stripped in a bid to rescue his colleague. An inquest later ruled the deaths had been accidental.

Exactly what happened remains a mystery but Gingrich theorized that either the propeller struck some standing timber and rocked the airboat, tipping the officers into the water, or Liddle fell out of the boat for another reason and Guenther tried to rescue him.

In the fall of 1967, C.O. Al Comfort suffered a miserably cold and lonely death on the shore of Shipsands Island, a bird sanctuary at the mouth of the Moose River. Aged in his mid-20s, Comfort had made for the island to collect crippled geese, an annual task undertaken by C.O.s to relieve the suffering of birds wounded by hunters. There, he beached his canoe, but a fast-moving tide swept in and carried the craft out to sea. Comfort made a desperate bid to get it back.

"It appears that he panicked," said Gerry English, fish and wildlife supervisor at Geraldton and Comfort's predecessor

FIGURE 7-3
Diving for fur trade artifacts in the French River, 1961. C.O.s Jim Sheppard (left) and Don Hughson pioneered the use of scuba diving equipment for fisheries management studies and other projects.

at Moosonee, "because he ran right out of his waders." Once his race against the tide had failed, Comfort returned to the shoreline to sit beside the willows along the bank where—cold, wet and without footwear—he died of hypothermia. An extensive land and air search soon located his canoe in the Moose River, but it was another two weeks before his frozen body, covered in seaweed, was discovered.

Just after freeze-up, a nearby resident gathering driftwood along the shore noticed a gun barrel sticking out of the ice. On closer inspection, he found the gun cradled by Comfort's body, which was huddled in the foetal position. Said English: "If Al could only have held on until the next low tide he could have walked back to the mainland. A ministry goose check station was located just half a mile along the shore."

At least two officers who died on duty—Otto Jordi and Kent Bibby—had their health give out. Otto Jordi, an officer based in Port Arthur during the late 1940s, suffered a heart attack as he pulled a toboggan laden with supplies across the snowy wastes of Shebandowan Lake. In his early 40s, Jordi was returning from an expedition checking traplines. When he failed to show up as expected, a search party found his body on the ice. He was buried wearing his full uniform and his casket was borne by fellow officers.

Kent Bibby collapsed and died in 1974 while he was checking night anglers on Agimak Creek, near Ignace, during the spring pickerel run. Bibby, thirty-eight years old, the son of long-serving warden Charlie Bibby, was a particularly hard-working officer with ten years' experience. He suffered from diabetes and had been diagnosed with a brain tumour about five years earlier.

"Kent knew the tumour would probably kill him, that he was living on borrowed time and perhaps that's why he pushed himself so hard," said his partner, Dave Penney. "He just loved the job and would regularly work fifteen-to-sixteen-hour days, seven days a week."

Treacherous winter conditions very nearly claimed the life of Ed Skuce, a legendary officer who served from 1930 to 1965. After falling through thin ice while checking anglers near Powassan during the early 1940s, he was saved, quite literally, by an air pocket and his trusty jack-knife!

When Skuce suddenly disappeared and failed to resurface, two men ran for help. On their return, there was still no sign of the warden who, as time ticked relentlessly on, was given up for dead. Ten full minutes elapsed before—miraculously—a tiny steel blade was spotted sawing through the ice. Having survived by breathing air trapped beneath the icy surface, Skuce was hauled to safety by disbelieving anglers.

Never one to boast of his exploits, Skuce was "almost overly shy," according to his son, Peter. Indeed, he was so reticent after his prolonged dunking in the frigid lake that, rather than return home, he went elsewhere to thaw out. "He didn't want my mother to worry about him," said Peter.

"In fact, my mother didn't learn of the event until it was reported in the *Powassan News*!"

The physical risks of a C.O.'s job can be drastically compounded when mechanical equipment is involved. "White" Jack Stewart—so called because of his snowy white hair—must have regretted driving his cruiser on frozen White Lake, near Renfrew, one fateful Saturday morning in February, 1962. Not that he had much choice. Few ministry personnel were equipped with snow machines in those days and it was common for C.O.s to drive on the icy surface of a lake to check anglers. Besides, there had been complaints about people using multiple lines to take more than their fair share of fish.

> **The physical risks of a C.O.'s job can be drastically compounded when mechanical equipment is involved.**

All went well until a snow squall suddenly whirled the wintry air into invisibility. Stewart, who was accompanied by a deputy, decided to seek refuge by driving off the lake, but snow had already covered his cruiser's tire tracks and he was soon lost and driving in wide circles.

Suddenly, there was an almighty crash. The cruiser had slammed into the rock face of an island named, coincidentally, Stewart's Island. Stewart was restrained by the steering wheel, but the impact threw the deputy through the windshield. Stewart climbed out of the cruiser, pulled his deputy back into the car, stuffed the shattered windshield with his parka, and removed his tunic jacket, wrapping it around his colleague. Then, ill-clad for the conditions, he set out unsteadily to get help.

Based at nearby Dacre, Stewart recognized the island and knew that people were not very far away. But, in shock from the unexpected collision, he once more became disoriented and fell headlong to the ice.

Meanwhile, someone had spotted the wrecked cruiser and the injured deputy and called for help. But now Stewart was missing. Once the squall had exhausted itself, an aircraft carrying C.O. Ken Shoenauer conducted a search and Stewart's prostrate figure was quickly spotted on the ice. When Shoenauer reached him, Stewart was conscious but incoherent and his ungloved hands were frozen. "All he was worried about," said Paddy Hogan, who served with Stewart as a young officer, "was the condition of the guy in the vehicle."

The deputy made a rapid recovery but Stewart was forced to book off work for six months and was never again able to close his hands fully. Three years later, he suffered heart failure while checking anglers on the Ottawa River and, in 1968, another heart attack killed him as he drove home from Pembroke District Office. "Everybody knew Jack Stewart," said Hogan, "and everybody thought the world of him."

In 1987, a helicopter crash claimed the life of Henry Kujala, a highly respected officer from Parry Sound. He was taking aerial photographs of pickerel spawning beds near Serpent Rapids on the Seguin River when the chopper in which he was riding veered into the river gorge. The pilot, David Buzzell, also lost his life. The downed blue and white helicopter containing the bodies of the two men was found in dense bush after an intensive four-day air and land search.

Kujala, forty years old, was a nineteen-year M.N.R. veteran who had started as a C.O. in Maple District, then moved to Parry Sound where he was promoted to wildlife management officer in 1983. Proud of his knowledge of wolf trapping, he was generally acknowledged as M.N.R.'s "wolfman." He also earned special respect for his working expertise with whitetail deer.

"Henry was earnest, honest, optimistic and good-natured," said John Macfie, former fish and wildlife supervisor at Parry Sound. "People who are the best at what they do are to be found in the front lines and that's where Henry was. The front runners get knocked out first." The high esteem in which Kujala was held was underscored by the crowd of more than 300 people—among them at least one former poacher—that turned out for his funeral.

Bernie Wall could easily have perished in a helicopter crash and he shuddered as he recalled the most perilous sixty seconds of his life. As a C.O. based at Nipigon in 1967, he was tagging moose on Wolfpup Lake, north of Dorion, on a windy July day when the accident happened. In those days, a helicopter pilot would spot a moose swimming in a lake or river and endeavour to position the pontoons of his machine on either side of the moose's back. The accompanying C.O. would then perch on a pontoon and place a tag to the moose's ear.

Mid-way through such an operation, Bernie Wall's helicopter struck a wave and the chopper overturned, throwing the pilot into the water. Wall, currently a wildlife management officer in Thunder Bay, was trapped upside down underwater for a full minute until he managed to undo his seatbelt and crawl out through the helicopter's smashed plexiglass bubble.

"I definitely thought my number was up," said Wall, who was presented with visions of his wife and son as, submerged, he struggled to free himself with one uninjured hand. "To this day, I find it hard to talk about the accident."

Wall and the pilot trudged eleven kilometres to the nearest road where, bloodstained, he flagged down a pulp truck. Too late, he realized he had left his C.O.'s hat behind and, six weeks later, a U.S. angler snagged his headgear and jumped to some grim conclusions. "I still have that hat as a memento," Wall chuckled. Ironically, C.O. Bill Sameluk had been selected for the moose tagging assignment but Wall insisted on doing the job because it lay in his patrol area. Shortly after the crash, the helicopter tagging method was abandoned by the province.

In another terrifying misadventure, C.O.s Lorne Hudson and Rick Parsons crashed into a wilderness lake in May, 1978, while on a routine air patrol checking trophy anglers. Their float plane failed to pull out of a

FIGURE 7-4
C.O. Henry Kujala died in a helicopter crash on the Seguin River, near Parry Sound, in 1987.

sideslip, struck Whiteclay Lake—seventy-five kilometres north of Armstrong—then somersaulted a couple of times before sinking in three metres of water with its doors open. The two officers made it to the surface, their lungs nearly bursting.

Momentarily, Hudson, who was based at Dryden as flying enforcement officer, and Parsons, based in Armstrong, clung to an upturned float of the plane before realizing the pilot had not escaped the wreck. Diving back into the chilled water, they found him belatedly striking for the surface. Nearby anglers, including Jim Crawford, chief of Minnesota's State Troopers, sped to the trio's rescue.

Parsons is apprehensive about flying to this day. "The accident was scary but it didn't really bother me at the time," he said. "It's crept up on me."

On countless occasions, C.O.s have placed themselves at risk in responding to humans and animals in distress. In the late 1940s, C.O. Roy Muma and deputy warden Earl Weaver had just started a morning patrol on the Niagara River when they spotted three people waving frantically aboard a cabin cruiser that was drifting rapidly towards the cataracts leading to Niagara Falls. The boat's engine had broken down and the anchor would not hold. The officers caught up with the drifting vessel, threw a rescue line to the stricken passengers and towed the boat to a nearby landing.

Shortly after this operation, the officers were returning along the East River when they saw two boys in a small rowboat, drifting downstream. The boys were using makeshift oars fashioned from tree branches with pieces of boarding nailed to the ends, while the oarlocks were two small bolts, bent and practically useless. Not realizing their close proximity to the Falls, the boys were towed to safety by the officers.

One cool spring evening in 1986, C.O.s Paul Dennis, Steve Aubry, Dan McKnight and fish and wildlife technician Cam McCauley travelled ninety-five kilometres from the Cochrane District Office to the Floodwood River where a cow moose had fallen through melting ice and was trapped between the shore and open water. An Abitibi logging watchman had spotted the stricken moose and called for help.

FIGURE 7-5
Moose rescue in Cochrane District. On left, the ice-enclosed cow is trapped between the shore and open water. C.O. Paul Dennis crawls over the melting ice to set her free. In the canoe are rescue team members Cam McCauley and Dan McKnight.

While Dennis changed into a wet suit, Aubry snowshoed out to the limits of the ice to assess the situation and the moose's condition. "She was exhausted and the ice had worn all the skin off the front of her neck," he said. "There was some blood, but no deep cuts."

McKnight, Dennis and McCauley paddled up the open portion of the river until they were facing the ice-enclosed cow. McCauley and McKnight began to break open a connecting channel with the canoe while Dennis crawled over the ice and sat down beside the moose with his legs dangling into the hole. "She let me hold her head in my lap and finally stopped struggling while the others finished opening the channel," he said. The moose was then roped and led out to open water. Much to the surprise of her rescuers, she swam strongly to the far shore before smashing through some ice and snow and disappearing into the bush.

FIGURE 7-6
C.O.s are called upon to assist with evacuations and access restrictions during forest fire emergencies. Here C.O. Tom Logan is describing a fire restriction to a concerned cottager.

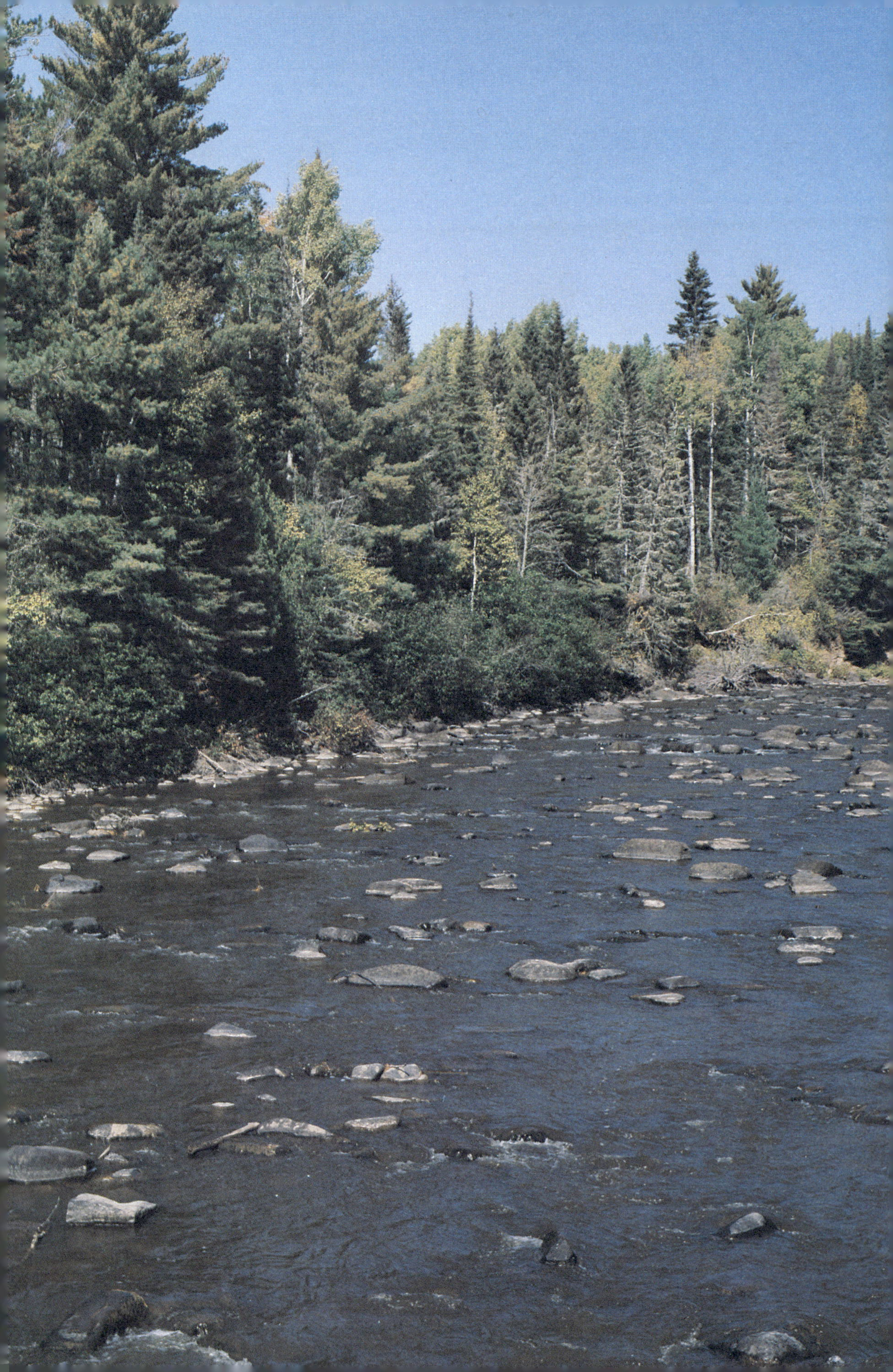

Chapter Eight: The Poaching Menace

Springtime had arrived, but one night in late March, 1968, was overcast and bitterly cold. A flurry of large, moist snowflakes blew against conservation officers Paddy Hogan and Jim Ives as they shivered beside a lonely barn overlooking Little Creek, a stream swollen with melting snow and ice. They were thinking hard about going home. Their wristwatches, after all, registered 1:30 a.m., and long, uneventful hours had been spent wandering from stream to stream, scouring Tweed District in search of poachers. Little Creek was in full flow and northern pike were running up from Hay Bay to spawn. It was a tempting spot to be lawless but there wasn't a soul to be seen. Even the most dedicated fish thieves, it seemed, were tucked up in bed.

Just then, the officers tensed instinctively as they saw the lights of a taxi moving down the road nearby. The cab pulled up a couple of hundred yards distant and two men wearing hip waders got out. The men waded into the stream and began walking towards the officers who soon heard the unmistakable sound of fish being speared, a fleshy sound interspersed with the harshness of steel striking rocks. As they drew closer, Hogan recognized one of them in the gloom, a young man, about 183 centimetres in height.

"He was a real bad dude," said Hogan. Both officers knew the man had a long criminal record

INSET: *Gotcha! C.O.s Ken Henry and Wray McQuay arrest a fish-spearing poacher at Duffins Creek, near Pickering. (Re-enactment: Spring, 1991)*

that included convictions for armed robbery and assaulting police officers. But that wasn't about to deter these patrolling C.O.s, whose tedious evening had suddenly burst into life. When the poachers were within a few yards, the officers flicked on their flashlights, bathing the culprits in brightness. Hogan asked them: "How are you doing tonight?"

Stunned, the "bad dude" responded with a stream of foul language. His accomplice, dropping a bag of fish, fled into the night with Ives in pursuit.

Hogan was on his own now. The taller man flourished his spear and backed into the stream. When Hogan told him "You might as well give yourself up," he only swore more liberally.

> **He kept pointing his spear at me and, all of a sudden, lunged forward with both hands and tried to thrust the blade into my stomach.**

"I waded into the water after him," Hogan recalled. "Blocks of ice were bumping off my waders. He kept pointing his spear at me and, all of a sudden, lunged forward with both hands and tried to thrust the blade into my stomach. I caught the blade in the palm of my hand. The spear snapped off and fell into the water."

Holding the broken shaft, the poacher turned and swam for the far bank, twenty-five metres away. Hogan swam after him. When his quarry clambered up the steep incline and charged blindly into a double layer of barbed wire fencing, Hogan did likewise. Desperately, they wrestled in the wire, the barbs tearing into their flesh. After jabbing Hogan in the temple with the spear's jagged shaft, the poacher extricated himself and jumped back into the stream. Hogan struggled to his feet and—from his vantage point high on the bank—leapt on his attacker's back, grabbing the hair of his head.

In the savagely cold stream, the wrestling match continued. "I never let go of his hair," said Hogan who, at 175 centimetres and seventy kilograms, was considerably shorter and lighter than his adversary. "At last I managed to hold his head under the water until he quit struggling. Then, with great difficulty, I dragged him up on shore and handcuffed him."

When Ives returned empty-handed from chasing the other poacher, he found his partner soaking wet and heaving with exhaustion, his face and hands streaming blood. The "bad dude" was taken to a cell at the O.P.P. detachment in Napanee sixteen kilometres away and Hogan's wounds were stitched and bandaged. Then, after Hogan had changed his clothes, the two C.O.s hit the trail once more. Their target: the home of the fleeing accomplice where they hoped to make a second arrest. He wasn't home but, as dawn broke, they picked him up trudging along the highway.

Both men were subsequently fined on a variety of charges, which included spearing and taking fish during the

FIGURE 8-1
Fish spearing doesn't pay! That's the message of this 1960 Ottawa Citizen photograph as D.C.O. Bill Bompas (left) and C.O. Wayne Robinson display pickerel, lanterns and spears seized from two men caught redhanded in the Jack River, near Richmond.

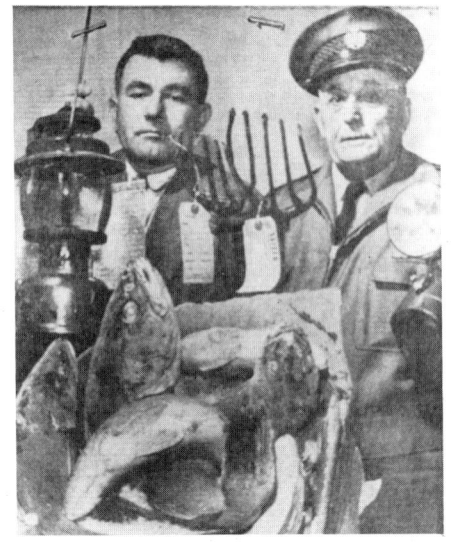

closed season. The man who plunged his spear into Paddy Hogan's hand was eventually sent to jail for six months for assaulting a peace officer. "All over a bunch of bony pike!" Hogan laughed. Not that the poachers were chastened by the drama at Little Creek. Three nights later C.O. Jack Sutton arrested the same men, once more, for spearing pike at night.

Whether the poacher is after a bagful of fish or a herd of moose, nothing galvanizes a C.O. more than the prospect of catching wildlife thieves red-handed. Historically, game wardens have always been the arch enemy of the poacher, whose greatest dread is the strident cry, "game warden!"

Long ago, veteran C.O.s will tell you, the poacher was often a poor, sometimes even principled, "gentleman" who killed in order to feed his family. The local warden knew such men personally and played out a traditional ritual of cat and mouse: the hunter and the hunted. Since the Second World War, however, "big business" has moved increasingly into the wild, raising the stakes. The lure of profit is strong. In April, 1986, it was said that a poacher working with a net could make as much as $5,000 in one night catching spawning rainbow trout.

Commercial operators, disregarding the delicate ecological balance, have slaughtered thousands of prized species for huge profits on the black market. These callous criminals seek not only deer, moose and fish, but also birds of prey, bears and reptiles—any creature, in fact, that has considerable economic value. C.O.s are the front line troops in this modern war against poaching, a war that must be won lest endangered species are wiped out and carefully tended reserves of game and fish are unduly depleted.

> **Whether the poacher is after a bagful of fish or a herd of moose, nothing galvanizes a C.O. more than the prospect of catching wildlife thieves red-handed.**

FIGURE 8-2
The early days of commercialization. Parry Sound C.O.s Walter McKinnon (left) and George Forson are pictured with pickerel taken from the Moon River at spawning time in April, 1950. The fish were confiscated en route to a Toronto restaurant.

The war has been going on for a long time now, although never, perhaps, with such intensity. Long ago, when the first wardens were on patrol, poaching seemed almost quaint by today's standards. Penalties that today might reach $100,000 or more for a highly organized ring of commercial operators were once little more than a wrist slap of a few dollars aimed, primarily, at stifling "a worthless class of loafing poachers" whose services were harnessed by "unscrupulous owners of timber camps and hotel keepers to supply them with illegal game," according to the 1902 report of the Ontario Game Commission.

Warden D.D. Young of the Quetico Game Reserve reported in 1913 that the smaller lumber camps were the greatest culprits, hiring men for $40 to $50 a month to keep them supplied with moose, deer and fish all winter. "If reports can be believed," Young added, "some lumber camps have actually used from fifty to 100 moose during the winter."

But the home population was not alone to blame. Non-residents toting costly equipment were the bane of early wardens in that they had both disrespect for the law *and* effective means of making a fast getaway. Leamington warden Charles Quallins complained in his report for 1892: "Time after time I have been disappointed in endeavouring to make arrests…simply because we could not compete in speed with the offenders who generally have fast sail, or steam yachts, and return to American waters before they can be arrested. These do more harm than the ordinary hunter, as they have swivel guns attached to their boats using a half-pound* of powder to about two pounds* of shot to a load, and often killing from fifteen to twenty ducks at one shot. They also have very strong field glasses, and can sight a man for a very long distance."

The following year, non-residents were still testing Quallins' patience. "The game law is no terror to the American poacher," he lamented, "but the licence of $25 is the thing he dreads, and he would rather run chances of getting caught than pay for his shooting in Canada."

Algonquin Park was a favourite plundering ground for poachers, particularly after the Department decided, in 1908, that beaver had become so numerous that park rangers should be allowed to do some supervised trapping within the boundary. Until 1920, annual fur sales of the rangers' collected skins were held, creating a storm of protest from trappers who were forbidden to work inside the park. The result was a massive outbreak in poaching and many was the ingenious scheme devised to outwit the rangers.

One poacher in particular would cross the cleared areas along the park borders using a pair of stilts carved underneath to resemble the hooves of a

---

* 2.2 pounds = 1 kilogram

deer. After getting past areas where snowshoe tracks might be discovered, he would dismount, hide the stilts in the underbrush and continue through the forest on snowshoes he had carried on his back. Another poacher packed the toes of his moccasins until they resembled heels, then wore his snowshoes backwards as he entered the park. The riddle of snowshoe tracks that always left yet never entered the park was sustained for a long time.

Algonquin Park's most famous poacher, Archie Belaney, was a lean, hawk-nosed young man from England who had read so voraciously about Canadian life in the bush that he decided to try the trapper's life for himself. For years, Belaney derived great pleasure in challenging and hoodwinking the authorities but, in the 1920s, he underwent a radical and romantic transformation to emerge as "Grey Owl," a beaver conservationist with a self-styled aboriginal ancestry. Grey Owl's books depicting the lives of his beaver friends "Rawhide" and "Jelly Roll" appealed to young people and pioneered the modern movement in conservation education.

Sales would be held all over the province of the equipment seized from poachers.

Sales would be held all over the province of the equipment seized from poachers. One such sale, in 1937, included: one hundred .22 calibre rifles, forty-four rifles of heavier calibre, forty-four single barrel shotguns, nineteen double barrel shotguns, seventeen fishing rods with reels, three tackle boxes with contents, twelve flashlights, five axes, three lamps and lanterns, twelve wooden duck decoys, ten haversacks and packsacks and six hundred animal traps.

The monthly bulletin of the Department of Game and Fisheries noted that the auction demonstrated the round-the-clock vigilance of the enforcement service and that "the life of a poacher is a precarious one." Yet only a few months earlier, the editors of the bulletin had expressed alarm that a

FIGURE 8-3
Grey Owl, a poacher who turned conservationist.

Attributed to William Oliver /
National Archives of Canada /
PA - 150000

growing poaching trend might undermine the ethics of hunters and anglers at large.

"There is a widespread impression among the general public," the bulletin observed, "that the Game and Fisheries laws are not serious contenders with other laws." This attitude was deplored as it led to wardens receiving "more abuse than sympathy" and incited excessive slaughter of game and fish by people who said to themselves: "I might as well have them as the poacher." The bulletin lectured its readers: "...the unvarnished truth is that taking fish or game illegally is just plain breaking one of the ten commandments...."

Then, as now, wardens would use moral persuasion wherever possible rather than force. Gananoque overseer Bob Sheppard has left behind an unusual account of how, in 1937, he persuaded a farmer to see the folly of his habitual poaching. On a routine visit of inspection, Sheppard was invited to stay for a chicken supper at the farmer's house before which the two men chatted in the barnyard:

"Now this man lived close to one of our finest trout lakes and was at that time an inveterate killer of trout during the spawning season. He had about 100 hens, so I said to him, 'Let's kill the whole bunch!' I said it so earnestly he half-believed I was serious and replied: 'What do you want to do that for?' I answered, 'Why, it's good fun.' He observed that he thought my idea a very crazy one. Right then, he and I went into a huddle over killing lake trout during the spawning season, with nets. Before we had finished the good chicken dinner, we had covered many angles of our conservation needs. I had often talked with this man before, but seemed never able to impress him properly until the chicken episode."

Before the last war, wardens would usually catch poachers by tracking them on foot, sometimes over many days and nights. "During the deer season I did a tremendous amount of walking," recalled Neil MacNaughtan, who served as warden in the Parry Sound area from 1920 to 1960. "That's the only way you got them. I'd leave home and not get back for ten days, maybe longer, and I'd have all these cases and they would plead guilty by mail and pay their fines."

Plead guilty and pay their fines! Contemporary C.O.s might be excused a twinge of envy at such a desirable state of affairs. But if most poachers caught fair and square would admit liability and pay up without a murmur in the "good old days," there were always exceptions to the rule. Fur buyer Mervyn Newman (a pseudonym) was such an exception, if only because he had so much at stake.

The date was June 2, 1938. Newman, a handsome young man dressed in the finest worsteds, had just stepped down from an eastbound passenger train at the C.N.R. railway station at Foleyet. He had walked only five paces, however, when he felt a tap on his shoulder. Turning, he found himself looking straight into the clear blue eyes of game and fishery overseer Lawrence Stanley Hemphill, a massively built individual often known as "Bull" or "Hemp" and considered by many to be the original "bull-o'-the-woods."

Hemphill had reason to suspect that Newman, though not a poacher himself, had been buying large quantities of fur from poachers and he wanted to see his books. Newman abruptly refused, and walked on. Hemphill grabbed him by the collar and flipped him upside down on the sooty platform. When Hemphill took his knee out of Newman's back and the fur buyer struggled to his feet, a soft-covered black book slipped from his coat pocket. Hemphill pounced on it.

The little black book, seemingly a ledger of sorts, was filled out in hieroglyphics, which "Bull" found indecipherable. Later, however, when the contents had been translated by an expert at the Royal Ontario Museum in Toronto, Hemphill—who was based at Elsas, twenty-four kilometres along the tracks—found himself sitting on a gold mine of information.

All the intricate dealings of illicit fur buying were spelled out in the most minute detail—the kinds and numbers of pelts purchased, the amount paid for each skin, the trappers or agents (many were railway employees) from whom the furs were purchased, and their addresses and code names. The book also disclosed where the pelts were hidden and their ultimate destination: Montreal.

The case against Newman came to trial at the Sudbury District Courthouse on July 25, 1938, and the Crown attorney proceeded with the most serious charge, that Newman did unlawfully ship the pelts of more than 490 fur-bearing animals—mainly beaver—outside Ontario without first paying the royalty, contrary to Section 29 of the Game and Fisheries Act. It was the largest game and fisheries case in Ontario thus far. Despite his initial resistance, Newman pleaded guilty and was fined a total of $16,395. That year, the Department of Game and Fisheries gathered together "a record assortment of confiscated furs" for public auction, which raised over $16,000. Almost forty-seven per cent of the beaver pelts for sale had once been in Newman's possession.

For Hemphill, who had started as an overseer in 1926, the Newman case was a crowning achievement. Much of his working life was spent patrolling the Chapleau Crown Game Preserve and it was there that the career of the man who for so long had been the bane of wrongdoers was grievously undone. In 1946, Hemphill himself was accused of being a poacher.

Acting on a telegram tip to Deputy Minister D.J. Taylor, overseers Charlie Bibby and Sam Nodwell tracked Hemphill's illegal trapping operation—run in conjunction with fellow warden Joe "Kid" Grant—to a shack inside the preserve. Subsequently, both Hemphill and Grant resigned.

Wardens who wind up as poachers, it cannot be emphasized too strongly, are rare indeed. More numerous are the number of C.O.s who have dabbled in poaching during adolescence to realize, later in life, the errors of their ways.

Back in 1936, thirteen-year-old Harry Gingrich (who retired in 1983 as Cambridge District enforcement coordinator) was spearing suckers with his elder brother, Clarence, one spring evening when C.O. Fred Merner stepped out of the bush, notebook in hand. Harry escaped with a warning and, years later, filled Merner's shoes after serving as his deputy. Carl Monk, who retired as regional enforcement specialist in Cochrane in 1985, met his wife Julie while she was acting as lookout for pickerel poachers. As a teenager, assistant provincial enforcement specialist Gord Black poached regularly with his father. He was never caught.

"I saw the light," Black said. "I saw that it wasn't fair—so I took the other side and became a conservation officer. When I started, I felt as though I owned every animal and every fish in my district. I was their mentor, their father, their keeper. And if anyone took one illegally I felt it like a slap in the face, like one of my own children had been stolen."

Like many a veteran, Carl Monk has apprehended poachers ranging in age from eight to eighty years old: "I've booked priests, judges, lawyers, even members of the U.S. Secret Service." Monk also knows from experience that the warden who wants to catch poachers in the act must be out and about at sunrise and sunset. "That's when the wildlife moves," he says. "That's when the poacher moves, too."

Monk cited an early morning escapade in April, 1952, that followed a tip leading him and fellow C.O. Auguste Wissell to Maskinonge Creek, at the west end of Lake Nipissing. "We paddled eight miles* by canoe to the creek from Monetville," he recalled. "We slept overnight in a tent with two inches* of snow outside. We got up at 4:30 next morning and paddled into the marsh and placed ourselves behind a muskrat house. When daylight came, the marsh exploded like an orchestra. There were blue herons, redwings, bitterns, the flip-flop of muskrat tails, the quacking of ducks—exciting stuff!

"Then I heard the splash and clump of some people in a punt followed by the thud of an animal—a muskrat, it turned out—being flung into the punt. Looking around, I saw that they were locals, checking their traps from a boat. We moved in to arrest them and, as we were talking, the guy

* 1.6 kilometres = 1 mile
2.5 centimetres = 1 inch

in the bow reached under the seat, pulled out the carcass of a great blue heron, twisted off a leg and started to eat it.

"We went back to their camp and it wasn't worth $1.98. There was a piece of ragged canvas, a couple of tins for plates, a couple of tins for mugs. The camp was forlorn, desperate, and so were they. They were on someone else's trapline and we could have charged them but we told them, instead, to lift their traps and leave. We gave them half a pound of bacon and some coffee."

Many are the occasions when wardens, their hearts melted by desperate circumstances, have dug into their own pockets to relieve the plight of unfortunates. Moreover, game and fish seized from poachers is frequently handed over for the enjoyment of those living in old folks' homes and other charitable institutions. Or to the needy at large. In July, 1939, more than two tonnes of fish were shared among hundreds of unemployed men after wardens seized a shipment that had been illegally transported from Quebec to Ottawa's Byward Market.

There is nothing more satisfying for a C.O. than to nab a poacher, literally, as he is going for the kill.

Years ago, elderly residents of the County Home at Beeton were beneficiaries of venison that would never have found its way to their stomachs had not C.O. Sandy Ellis, who worked in the Lake Simcoe area from 1945 to 1966, been invited to supper at a poacher's house. Tipped off that shots had been fired in the Bradford marsh overnight, Ellis visited a number of possible suspects accompanied by his son, Jack, who takes up the story:

"It was about dinner time when we arrived at one particular place. The owner of the house and his wife were very friendly. They called 'Sandy' by his first name and invited us to share in their 'roast of beef.' On the first bite, my Dad knew it was venison they were serving but did not say anything until after the meal. He then thanked the hosts for the delicious meal and told them that, venison being out of season, he would have to search the place for the carcass unless they could save him the effort by producing it.

"After some fast excuses and stories, the fellow decided, since his stories weren't going over too well, to take us outside to the back of his place where, sure enough, a freshly butchered deer was hanging from a tree. The moral of the story would be: Never serve the game warden venison when it's out of season!"

There is nothing more satisfying for a C.O. than to nab a poacher, literally, as he is going for the kill. Carl Monk fondly remembers sneaking up in a canoe behind a man who was shooting at fish in Lake Nipissing to place his hand on the man's shoulder, feeling the gun recoil. Ninety-year-old Vern Windsor, who served as a C.O. during the 1940s, recounted a similar adventure that took place before dawn at Burleigh Falls: "Through the rain, I saw a man fishing at the far end of the falls. He had seen me and the car so I decided to drive by him really fast and make my way back. I turned out the headlights. I knew he wouldn't hear me because of the noise from the falls. I came right up behind him and waited for him to cast. Then I put my hand on his shoulder. He sure jumped and turned white!"

Mervin Windover, who lives among the Kawartha Lakes near Buckhorn, knows what it's like to be caught napping by a game warden. Describing himself as a reformed poacher, Windover has been convicted at least ten times for poaching, has had two guns confiscated and has paid roughly $3,000 in fines.

"As a boy I would go out with my Dad and we would shoot whatever we needed," he said. "It says in the Bible that game was put on this earth in abundance for food. You don't eat just two weeks of the year." Windover's father, Clarion, was a professional poacher who died at the age of eighty-one. Possessing extraordinary intuition, he was never caught—even though neighbours "squealed" on him in hope of gaining the $5 fee paid to local informants during the 1930s. On one occasion, Clarion "had a feeling" that a warden was waiting to arrest him on his return from an illegal hunting expedition along the Squaw River. After taking a different way home, he learned that the warden, and his informant, had been lying in wait for him.

Mervin Windover was shooting a rifle at the age of six and was just ten years old when he filled his first order as a poacher—for a pair of partridges. He went on to poach deer, ducks and fur-bearing animals but retired from poaching when he gave up drinking. "Poaching was an easy way to make money to buy booze," he said. "When I quit drinking I thought: 'Life's too valuable to go on like this.'"

Looking back, he feels he was well-treated by his nemesis, the game warden. "I wouldn't have the warden's job for a million dollars," he said. "They've got the lousiest job in the world."

Exactly when poaching turned into a big business proposition is anybody's guess. Mervyn Newman, certainly, had commercialized the theft of fur bearers back in the 1930s. But organized rings formed with intent to capitalize on Ontario's wildlife have only been exposed in relatively recent times.

Commercialization emerged as a major threat to Ontario's fish and wildlife populations in the 1970s. Large-scale poaching operations raked in huge profits by harvesting quantities of animals, deer especially, for sale on the black market. Largely to combat this trend, two special investigators were appointed as a roving team in April, 1983. In September, 1986, a Special Investigations Unit was created, working out

> "It says in the Bible that game was put on this earth in abundance for food. You don't eat just two weeks of the year."

FIGURE 8-4
Reformed poacher Mervin Windover: "I wouldn't have the warden's job for a million dollars."

of an unmarked Cambridge warehouse under the leadership of John Todd. On staff were a secretary and three officers adept at intelligence gathering and undercover sleuthing.

A special investigations operation called Operation Polar Bear led to the arrest of a tourist agent based in Waterdown, Ontario, who was smuggling polar bear hides into the United States. The agent was organizing Arctic polar bear hunts at $18,000 a trip, then contravening the Export and Import Permits Act by selling the treated bearskins to the hunters.

After a giant mounted polar bear was discovered by U.S. agents in Texas, C.O. George Humphrey began a covert investigation in tandem with the U.S. Fish and Wildlife Service. A network of polar bear hunters was identified across the United States and the Ontario agent was arrested in St. Paul, Minnesota, where he was about to address the Safari Club International on his organizational exploits.

The agent's home and business were later searched and thousands of pages of documents were seized, including a letter to U.S. hunters telling them how to age documents so as to smuggle in the bearskins. He was jailed for thirty days in the United States and ordered to pay a $20,000 fine. In Hamilton, Ontario, in November, 1988, he was fined $70,000—the largest penalty paid in Canada by an individual in answer to wildlife-related charges.

In 1988, one of the biggest undercover operations ever undertaken in Canada was launched to counter massive poaching of deer on Manitoulin Island. A special investigation was aimed mainly at "jack lighters"—poachers who shoot deer after "freezing" them in the beams of powerful headlights or flashlights. It was estimated that the annual toll of illegally

In 1988, one of the biggest undercover operations ever undertaken in Canada was launched to counter massive poaching of deer on Manitoulin Island.

FIGURE 8-5
Illegal spoils. C.O. John Diebolt is pictured with white-tail deer purchased by C.O.s during a covert investigation undertaken in 1989.

slaughtered deer on Manitoulin Island had risen to more than 1,000 animals.

Coordinated by C.O.s Ian Anderson and Gary Couillard, the probe involved a total of fifty-seven officers. Initially, Anderson and his partner, John Diebolt, gathered intelligence on a wide range of suspects after realizing that certain individuals were killing deer for sale in urban centres across Ontario. Tips and information from the public aided the investigation—a far cry from the early 1970s when Manitoulin warden Terry Matz received a barrage of harassing phone calls and was greeted by the sight of deer heads and entrails strewn across his lawn.

By the end of the investigation, early in 1990, 1,796 kilograms of deer meat from forty-one animals had been purchased by undercover officers and thirty-five people had been charged with illegal hunting. In all, the suspects were charged with some 300 offences under the Game and Fish Act. Quantities of vehicles and firearms were seized.

In 1990, the climax of a two-year investigation called Operation Border Waters led to more than 300 charges being laid against Canadian and non-resident hunters and anglers for a wide variety of poaching offences.

In 1990, the climax of a two-year investigation called Operation Border Waters led to more than 300 charges being laid against Canadian and non-resident hunters and anglers for a wide variety of poaching offences. After monitoring several hunting and fishing operations in the Lake of the Woods, undercover officers from Ontario and Minnesota documented a host of violations ranging from hunting on a game preserve and selling deer to using power boats to hunt waterfowl and taking inordinate quantities of fish.

Operation Outback in 1988 zeroed in on taxidermists across the province. A covert investigation conducted by M.N.R. investigator Al Giesche and Corporal David Hill of the R.C.M.P. led to the conviction of thirty-five taxidermists who had illegally purchased wildlife ranging from pickerel to moose heads and then resold their acquisitions after turning them into decorative items. Approximately $100,000 worth of mounted wildlife was seized and fines totalled $36,000. "If people want a rug or a trophy specimen, they won't necessarily kill the animal or fish themselves," said Giesche. "The demand is there."

The demand is there, too—several million dollars worth of demand—for endangered birds of prey, as an investigation titled Operation Falcon quickly discovered in 1984. In the course of their inquiries, Cambridge C.O.s Ron Jean-Marie, Peter Meerveld and deputy C.O. Carolyn Moore found that winged predators and their eggs were being taken illegally from nests all over North America and Europe and smuggled into Ontario. From Ontario, using false documentation, they would be exported as domestically bred birds to states in the Persian Gulf. Profits were phenomenal. The gyrfalcon, for example, traded for more than $65,000 (U.S.) to buyers in the Middle East.

Working in close cooperation with the U.S. Wildlife Service and the R.C.M.P., officers placed a small number of bird dealers under surveillance and swooped to make arrests when they had gathered sufficient evidence. In time, the investigation turned out to be the biggest wildlife enforcement initiative in North American history. It focused on more than 150 people in Ontario, other Canadian provinces, fourteen U.S. states and West Germany. In Ontario, one suspect was convicted and fined $20,000, but the kingpin of the operation—who faced thirty-five charges—jumped bail in 1985 and fled to Saudi Arabia. So far as anyone knows, he's still there. Said Jean-Marie: "Ounce for ounce the proceeds are more lucrative for smuggling endangered birds than they are for smuggling drugs. The penalties are less harsh and the chances of getting caught are fewer."

Operation Falcon was not the only time C.O. Jean-Marie

"Ounce for ounce the proceeds are more lucrative for smuggling endangered birds than they are for smuggling drugs."

FIGURE 8-6
A peregrine falcon was one of the winged predators offered for sale by racketeers investigated during Operation Falcon.

and deputy C.O. Moore have teamed up. Between 1984 and 1988, they joined ranks with U.S. investigators to expose an international smuggling ring dealing in rare eagle feathers. More than 1,500 eagle and vulture feathers worth about $33,000 were seized in Operation I.C.E. (International Commerce in Eagles). Most of the feathers were being exported from the United States to Canada and sold to aboriginal people and non-aboriginal art collectors.

"We're talking a lot of birds," said Jean-Marie, of Cambridge District, estimating that several hundred rare and endangered eagles must have been slaughtered. After the officers posed as buyers and paid $4,000 for two headdresses and a long "trailer" of eagle feathers, individuals in Ontario and the United States were fined. It was discovered that some feathers originated in China and Tibet, were imported into the United States as goose feathers, and then sold as eagles' plumage. In fact, the feathers were plucked from old world vultures (a species near extinction) while the birds were still alive, according to testing at Washington's Smithsonian Institution.

Poachers' brutality feeds yet another booming trade—the traffic in deer and moose antlers and bears' gall bladders and claws. Economic growth, rising personal incomes and increasing trade opportunities in Asian countries have produced rising demand for traditional medicines and aphrodisiacs. These commodities require animal parts that, after being harvested in Ontario, fetch inflated prices in the Orient.

Bear gall bladders, which are used for folk medicines to relieve cancer and heart conditions, sell for roughly $100 at source but can be worth $2,000 in Asia, according to Rick Stankiewicz, enforcement coordinator in Whitney. Ontario's black bears—fodder for this trade—have been found gutted and mutilated, with their paws hacked off. Their claws are sought as jewellery items.

In a 1990 investigation, an undercover officer purchased antlers—raw material for aphrodisiacs—as well as bear parts. Charges followed against twelve tourist operators and guides from the Algonquin Park area. "This case is the tip of an iceberg," said Stankiewicz, who planned the operation. Underscoring his comment is the disclosure that thirty-two kilograms of dried black bear galls from an estimated 1,000 black bears went down in the Irish Sea aboard the Air India Boeing 747 that exploded en route from Toronto to New Delhi—killing 329 people—in June, 1985. The shipment had a retail value of close to $1 million.

There is no sign that the poaching menace is abating. On the contrary, a 1991 report prepared for the Ontario Wildlife Working Group by John

Johnson, an enforcement specialist in Aurora, insisted that "there is no species and no area in Ontario that is untouched by poaching." The report called for the establishment of a province-wide Report-A-Poacher programme to operate around the clock and maintained that penalties for commercial violations were still too lenient.

The battle against poaching has become a universal struggle. Wildlife is under siege worldwide and, as special investigator Ben Attard pointed out, "There is a great need to look at wildlife protection from a global standpoint. We must work together with other agencies to prevent imports as well as exports of all types of endangered species—ours is a common heritage."

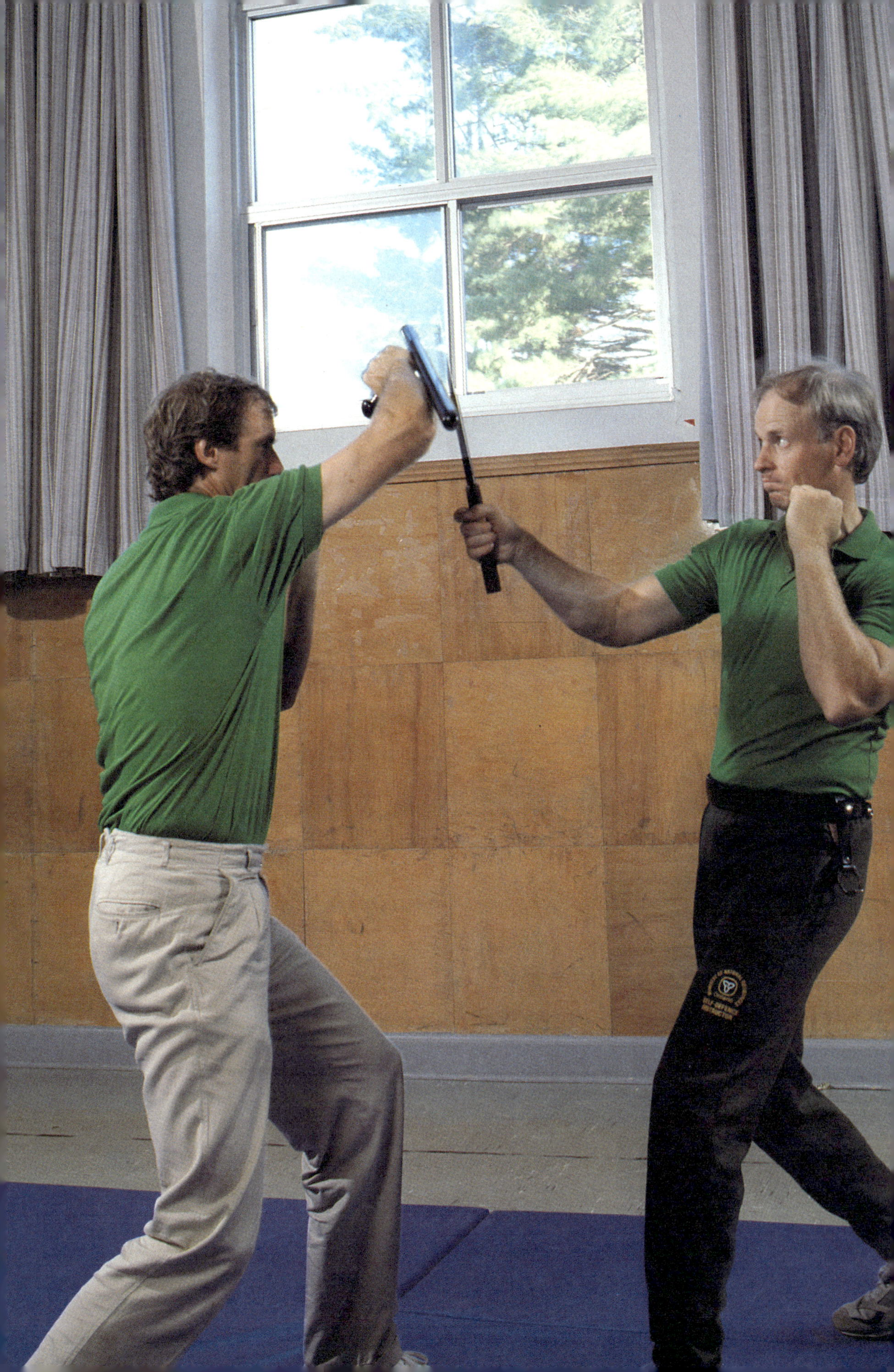

Chapter Nine: In School at Last

The recruitment of a game warden used to be a simple matter. Hiring was likely so long as the candidate was "a gentleman of good character," with a strong physique and an aptitude for rugged living. Once employed, the new recruit received no training of any kind. After a rudimentary lecture on the game and fish laws, he was dispatched into a designated sector of the wilderness with instructions to maintain intermittent contact with his superiors at Queen's Park. Only God and the warden knew how the job would be accomplished.

As time went by, more thought was given to the qualities that every warden should possess. In his rigorous examination of the Game and Fisheries Department from 1909 to 1911, Commissioner Kelly Evans mulled over the employment profile before stating that the principal requirements should be "good character and sobriety, health, energy, strength, fearlessness, tact, thorough knowledge of the game laws and fishery regulations, and education sufficient to read and write." After further deliberation, he added: "...knowledge of the denizens of the woods, their characteristics and habits, thorough expertness in the handling of a canoe, and experience in life in the woods and woodcraft, should be considered indispensable attainments."

Living up to these expectations was not so easy and by the time a further study of the field service

INSET: *Classroom instruction is an integral part of training.*

LEFT: *C.O. Jim Fry (right) teaches martial arts at the Leslie M. Frost Centre in Dorset, the hub of specialized C.O. training. His instruction in self-defense and hand-to-hand combat hones and upgrades C.O.s' skills.*

was undertaken in 1930, the reporting committee was concerned that "some more definite means should be applied of ascertaining by external inquiry to what extent a field officer is or is not likely to be efficient." That magic word—"training"—was then mentioned in a recommendation that the service be composed of "young, active men with proper physique and qualifications *who can be especially trained for the work*."

Training, however, was not to be introduced for at least another fifteen years when the first courses for wardens were held directly after the Second World War. At the outbreak of the First World War, all wardens leaving for the front lines were told that their jobs would be kept open. The same promise was made as hostilities began in 1939 and, because the Department expanded as well as gave priority to returning soldiers, sailors and airmen, veterans swelled the ranks of Ontario's field service at war's end.

By March, 1947, veterans made up at least eighty per cent of Ontario's field force of 177 wardens—an increase of thirty per cent since the war. Toughened by conflict and privation, they were consummate outdoor lovers, fiercely independent and not overly fond of studying. Soon after they signed up, the Department mounted an intensive four-day course of "legal and administrative instruction" to prepare them for the increasing complexity of the job. Training, though barely a consideration for more than half a century, was suddenly a beacon illuminating the way to the future.

In 1946, Ontario's first Forest Ranger School opened its doors at Dorset—a joint enterprise between the Department of Lands and Forests and the Faculty of Forestry at the University of Toronto. Located beside Lake St. Nora and the 4,047-hectare University Forest, the school was dubbed "Ontario's School of the Outdoors" and became a second home for all who worked, in varying capacities, in the forests. A thirty-three-week general diploma course quickly established itself as a "must" for aspiring game wardens and special law enforcement and fish and wildlife courses were designed to refine the theoretical and practical capabilities of experienced officers. Studies ranged from stream measurement to tree identification, from forest protection to camp construction.

Game wardens Harold Bailey of Gore Bay and Sudbury's Lawrence Michon were among the school's first seven graduates. "You men in the field are the backbone of the department," declared school director Pete McEwan in presenting their diplomas. "While there have been great advancements along technical lines in recent years in the department, I still believe it is the men in the field who do the actual work—always have, and always will."

Although the accent at Dorset was on "learning by doing," not every lesson was an enjoyable experience. Many wardens had received only the

> **Studies ranged from stream measurement to tree identification, from forest protection to camp construction.**

most basic education and felt uncomfortable at returning to the classroom. Len Cote of Marten River, for example, found the sedentary studies a nightmare, referring to the school as "Knowledge College." "I only went to school for two days in my life," Cote would say. "They were the two days I took the place of my brother when he was sick!"

Biologist Bruce Collins, who taught at the school from 1964 to 1973, recalled that many of the established C.O.s didn't like taking notes. "They thought that learning with books and paper was a crock," he said. "But these were guys who had come out of the bush reluctantly."

In any case, training for C.O.s acquired little sophistication before the 1970s. Mainly, the younger officers learned from the older ones and that was that. When Carl Monk was accepted as a warden in 1951, a telegram instructed him to report to Queen's Park for a one-week course. There, he and several other recruits were subjected to an information barrage on fish and wildlife management, report compilation and the dos and don'ts of enforcement.

"We covered an awful lot of ground," said Monk, "but none of us knew where we were going to end up. That is, until Friday afternoon when the course supervisor put the names of different places in a beret and passed it around the room. I drew Sault Ste. Marie and boarded the overnight train going north. A C.O. met me at the station the next morning and that afternoon I was on a local ferry dock checking American fishermen. That's when I made my first arrest—charging two fishermen with catching double their limit of pike. The fun and games had started...."

The Forest Ranger School's thirty-three-week course was a good primer, but for more than twenty years, most C.O.s had no formal training

> "They thought that learning with books and paper was a crock."

FIGURE 9-1
The imposing lecture hall of the Leslie M. Frost Natural Resources Centre.

FIGURE 9-2
Peter Kataquapit, Ontario's first aboriginal C.O.

FIGURE 9-3
Margaret Reed, pictured in 1981—a year after she was named Ontario's first woman C.O.

in enforcement itself until several years *after* being hired. In 1964, a three-week law enforcement course was introduced at the Ontario Police College, Aylmer, but initially the only beneficiaries were C.O. supervisors. In time, however, ministry instructors were brought in and field officers were sent for tuition in how to handle their mushrooming responsibilities.

As coaching grew in importance, the basic requirements for a C.O.'s job became more stringent. By 1968, a candidate had to have achieved Grade 12 or better and have graduated from a forest ranger school. He had to be between twenty-two to thirty-five years old, at least 170 centimetres, and weigh a minimum of 66 kilograms.

Simultaneously, there was a trend towards greater liberalization that dissolved the invisible barriers restricting a C.O.'s job to males of white, European heritage. In 1960, Peter Kataquapit became the first native person to be hired as a C.O.

Kataquapit was running a general store in Moosonee frequented by local officers when warden Andy Gagnon offered him a job. "I can't be sure why he chose me," said Kataquapit. "But I was reliable and...I knew they needed help with interpreting, as ninety per cent of the people in the Moosonee area speak Cree."

Kataquapit concentrated on trapline management work and moose and caribou surveys. Being aboriginal in a predominantly aboriginal region complicated his role as enforcer. "It was difficult and involved a lot of personal conflict," he said. He argued that the job became harder when aboriginal people started getting into politics. Although Kataquapit quit his job as a C.O. in 1973, he had blazed a trail that encouraged others to follow in his footsteps.

The trail-blazer for women C.O.s was Margaret Reed, who triumphed over twenty-four male applicants to become a Chatham District conservation officer in May, 1980. "The first few years were really tough because my male colleagues tended to relate to women in a stereotypical way," said Reed. "It took a lot of work and trust on everybody's part for me to be taken seriously as an individual who could be counted on in a tense working situation."

As Ontario's first female C.O., Reed was subjected to endless ribbing in the office as well as all kinds of chauvinist pranks. But Reed weathered the storm to earn respect in the field and a reputation for toughness in the community. "For a man or a woman," said Reed, "this job can be the greatest in the world."

In 1991, there were three women C.O.s in the province aside from Margaret Reed—Anne Kirk of Lindsay, Barb McMullen of Ignace and Joan Hubay of Kenora. Said Hubay: "It's about time people started looking at the job for what it is rather than whether it is a male or female job. I don't want people to presume that women have to be one of the guys. I've realized that I can retain my femininity and do the job."

In recent years, every announced C.O. vacancy has been fiercely contested, especially in southern Ontario. Fifty or more applications for a C.O.'s job is not unusual. In October, 1989, 300 people applied for a bilingual position in Algonquin Park.

Many would-be officers work voluntarily for years as deputy C.O.s, applying time and again for full-time positions before finally landing a job. To increase their employment prospects, some determined applicants complete training of their own in advance of the job interview. For example, after having applied unsuccessfully for thirty different C.O. positions between 1981 and 1987, Ken Snowden received special permission from the M.N.R. to attend the three-week enforcement course at the Ontario Police College during his vacation. The course cost him $800, as well as a holiday, but turned out to be a wise investment. In June, 1988, he applied for another C.O.'s position at Maple—and got the job.

General diploma courses were switched to Sir Sandford Fleming College, Lindsay, in 1968, and later, other community colleges joined in mounting two, three and four-year programmes. The Leslie M. Frost Natural Resources Centre (the Dorset school renamed in honour of the former Ontario premier), meanwhile, concentrated on more specialized training, honing law enforcement skills and using the outdoor classroom for action-oriented, trial-and-error exercises. As much realism as possible would be created in, for example, simulating rowdyism in a provincial park and conducting search-and-seizure operations and courtroom trials. Consistently, the principle has been to learn by active participation.

Ralf Aldrich, Ontario's first provincial enforcement specialist from 1976 to 1979, "got the ball rolling," as he put it, to upgrade training. His successor, Cliff Copeland, strengthened the initiative. Since Dale Gartley took over in 1982, training activity has expanded far beyond the basic staples of enforcement and fish and wildlife. Furthermore, the earlier reliance upon the Ontario Police College has given way to training coordinated by the M.N.R. at the Frost Centre. Today, the Frost Centre is the engine room of C.O. training.

Firearms training started in earnest in 1980, C.O.s being required to reach a basic level of marksmanship in yearly shoots. Before then, individual officers were relied upon to train themselves with as much help as they could get from their local O.P.P. detachment. In the past decade, however, there has been a determined effort to make Ontario's C.O.s increasingly proficient with their .38 Smith and Wesson revolvers. In 1983, new marksmanship awards were introduced—the "crossed" and "silver" revolvers for officers scoring 400 and 475 points respectively out of 500 in the annual firearms test. Targets were constantly updated, as was the "bible" of

> **As much realism as possible would be created in, for example, simulating rowdyism in a provincial park and conducting search-and-seizure operations and courtroom trials.**

straight shooting—M.N.R.'s *Firearms Training Manual*.

In 1988, ace marksman Ted Biggs set to work training twenty-two firearms instructors across the province. Said Biggs, a Kenora C.O.: "I would pit our instructors against any police instructors in the country." As a vote of confidence in their prowess, the level of difficulty for qualification in the firearms test was increased in 1991.

As with firearms, C.O.s are tested each year in their ability to use side-handle and expandable batons. Jim Fry, a Ministry martial arts expert, leads the way in self-defence training, which extends to hand-to-hand combat and pressure point instruction. "We've come a long way in a very short time," he said.

Mandatory level one and level two law enforcement courses are currently held at the Frost Centre for C.O.s in their first year of employment. Before taking the level three course—which teaches management and investigative skills as well as serving as a refresher on key topics—an officer must have five years' experience. Level four is devoted to special investigations; trainees must have both an interest in and an aptitude for pursuing undercover work.

There is a basic and advanced prosecutor's course and a forensic accounting course to enable officers to trace paper trails through labyrinthine bookkeeping. Workshops are held, too, on a wide variety of subjects—from commercial fishing enforcement to the Charter of Rights and Freedoms. More and more, training videos are being produced to amplify and illustrate the instruction at hand.

In August, 1990, water safety courses for C.O.s were staged by Alex Cumming, vice-president of Lifestar International, a private company specializing in safety training. Cumming has since held courses in ice safety, vessel operation and navigation.

FIGURE 9-4
C.O.s in training, hard at work in this classroom scene at the Ontario Police College, Aylmer.

FIGURE 9-5
Learning the workings of the law. C.O. Mark Wickham (foreground) takes part in a mock trial held at The Old Bailey Courtroom in Cobourg's Victoria Hall.

"We do not believe in straight theory," said Cumming, underscoring the Frost Centre's values. "The idea is to learn the theory and then do the techniques because it is only when you actually do something that you learn what might be encountered."

In demonstration of his seriousness, Cumming ordered a two-and-a-half-metre square hole cut in icy Lake St. Nora in February, 1991, and had C.O.s clambering into rubberized immersion suits to practise self-rescue techniques in the frigid water. Then he invited officers to jump into the lake without insulated gear so that they might test both the chill and their responses.

The stresses and strains of a warden's life have been addressed in training since 1982 during stress management courses run by Al Montgomery, previously an O.P.P. officer, now a peer counsellor. He not only leads courses, but also runs stress workshops for C.O.s and their spouses and conducts individual counselling.

"C.O.s are keenly aware that they are the buffer, that they are the last line of defence," Montgomery said, indicating one of the most stressful aspects of the job. Alan Farrer, 1991 president of the Ontario Conservation Officer's Association observed, "C.O.s are often caught between their loyalty to the resources and their loyalty to the government. But the resources come first—that's where their strongest commitment lies." Other stresses involve the dangers of facing armed violators, verbal aggression and lack of empathy from some resource users, perceived inequities in the judicial system and the pressure of peer bonding with other C.O.s. "Part of what I attempt to do," said Montgomery, "is to try to allow the officers to be real people for a change and say real things to themselves that they would not normally say because of the C.O. image."

One of the latest courses to be introduced has an ancient theme: wilderness survival. The course is the brainchild of C.O. Art Zimmerman, who has lived all his life in the wilds and whose survival knowledge springs from experience. Several times, he was flown into remote areas of northern Ontario and left there longer than planned because deteriorating weather conditions prevented the aircraft's return. Zimmerman feels his course is particularly relevant today as more and more young C.O.s, hired straight from school, have scant knowledge of survival techniques.

Lorne Hudson, a veteran officer who instructs in law, special investigations and enforcement, has been made abruptly aware of the difference between academic learning and practical know-how. "We have people taking C.O.s' courses who have never caught a fish, who have never trapped or hunted," he said. "We have people who have never driven a boat or a vehicle with a standard gearshift." Hudson takes great satisfaction in tutoring such novices in the practical side of life once the books have been put away for the day. "It's amazing how fast most of them learn," he added.

Despite the great strides made in training over the past decade, Dale Gartley insists: "We are only half-way there." Plans exist for the expansion

> Other stresses involve the dangers of facing armed violators, verbal aggression and lack of empathy from some resource users, perceived inequities in the judicial system and the pressure of peer bonding with other C.O.s.

FIGURE 9-6
"Come on in, the w-w-water's f-f-f-fine!" C.O.s Terry O'Neill (left) and Duncan Hall practise self-rescue techniques in frigid water as part of survival training at the Leslie M. Frost Natural Resources Centre in February, 1991.

of existing training regimens, as well as for initiatives in public relations, public speaking, management duties, counselling and the training of instructors. "Things are moving so fast in the world of law enforcement that we must constantly update our courses, training plans and manuals," said Gartley. "And we must be constantly thinking about how better to get across the message of habitat and wildlife protection."

In May, 1987, the Kenrick Report on the role of Ontario's C.O.s maintained that the greatest advancement in C.O.s' evolution over the past decade "has been the enhancement of enforcement training." Certainly, those who well remember cruder approaches to training are proud of the new-look outfit. "We've got the best trained officers in North America" declared Aubrey Gostlin, the first C.O. to instruct at the Ontario Police College. He paused before adding reflectively: "…maybe even the world."

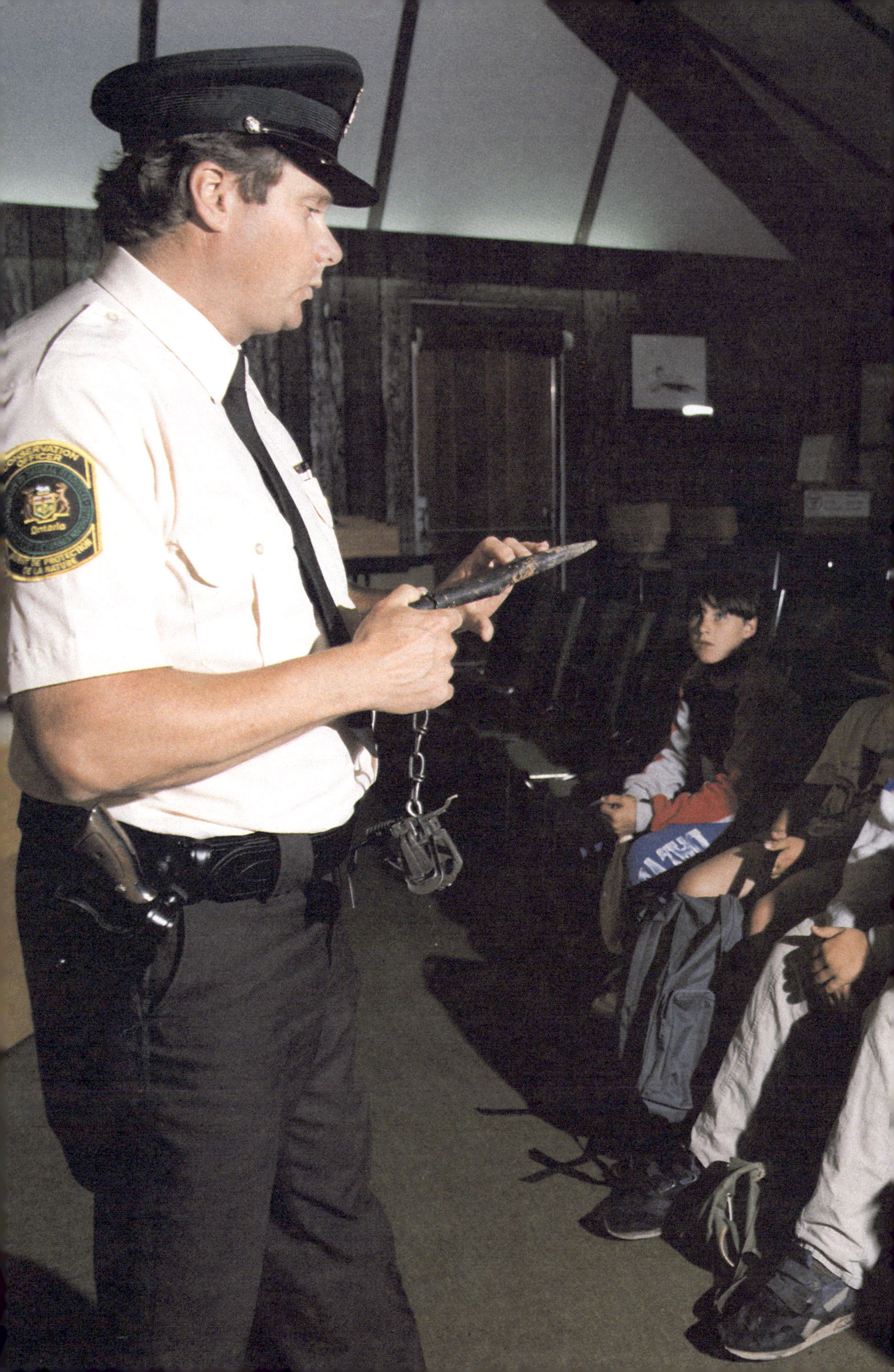
CONSERVATION OFFICER
Ontario

Chapter Ten: Helping Hands

Few in number for the huge task of safeguarding more than one million square kilometres of lands and waters, C.O.s have been fortunate in being able to call upon an enthusiastic army of helping hands. Support has come from many sources, but the most persistent contribution has been supplied by individuals whose affection for wildlife and the outdoors has prompted them to toil unstintingly in the cause of conservation. Several thousand of these dedicated people have proudly carried the badge of deputy warden.

The first deputies—392 of them—started work back in 1892 as unpaid volunteers, although they did receive half the fine paid by anyone convicted as a result of their efforts. Nevertheless, any deputy who lost a case was required to pay court costs, leaving him not only unpaid, but out-of-pocket too!

The following diary entries, made by Huntsville deputy warden Charles Chapman in the winter of 1892/93, illustrate the arduousness of the daily round:

Saturday, November 5th: *Pushed on up river to crossing place; water too high; went on up to still water and built a raft and crossed. Found that some ill-disposed person had set fire to my log shanty and burnt it and its contents, owing to my holding office of Deputy-Warden.*

INSET: *A conservation officer explains the raising of fish in a hatchery to pupils from Burnt River School visiting Victoria county forest Headquarters, Lindsay District, in January, 1964.*

LEFT: *Huronia District C.O. Sid Small carries the message of environmental care into the classroom.*

Tuesday, January 10th: *I left Hunstville at 4.30 a.m. with an Indian sleigh, pair of blankets, axe, rifle, food, snowshoes etc. with one Chris A. Peacock as companion. Cold, sharp wind. Thermometer registered 42 below zero... Took east road to Grassmere 6 miles*, thence north-east 4 miles* to Field's Corners. Here Peacock rued coming; said he was played out, took his things and left me to push on alone... Tired out. Day's tramp 19 miles*.*

Wednesday, January 18th: *I was kept awake all night by the howling of wolves. My feet were so cold this morning that I had to crawl on my hands and knees till I found dry wood to rekindle my fire.*

The original deputies were appointed on the recommendation of county judges, police magistrates, gun clubs, county wardens and other community leaders.

The original deputies were appointed on the recommendation of county judges, police magistrates, gun clubs, county wardens and other community leaders. The Board of Game Commissioners wanted men who were "intimately acquainted with the game districts and the residents of the neighbourhood and would naturally hear more of what was going on than a stranger could possibly do."

By 1896, there were 460 deputy wardens but they were not all working as hard as Huntsville's Charles Chapman. In fact, Chief Warden Edwin Tinsley reported that the majority "simply do nothing" for fear of offending their neighbours and because they were nervous about the possibility of finding themselves in arrears after testifying in court. In 1900, when the Ontario Game Commission announced that all deputy game wardens must take an oath of office binding them to discharge their duties honestly, their numbers slumped from 527 to 209.

But in succeeding years, after deputies' appointments were placed in the hands of wardens, the force grew both in numbers and commitment. Many deputies joined up from the ranks of the growing number of fish and game protective associations; others were enlisted on the recommendation of municipal councils of townships established as regulated game preserves.

On their own, game wardens simply could not handle the staggering workload and the vast distances involved. This was acknowledged in the 1930 report of a special committee on the game-fish situation, which expressed the "improbability" that the Department of Game and Fisheries could maintain the protective service unaided and asked that greater use be made of club memberships "for protective and conservational purposes."

By 1960, there were 1,400 deputy wardens in Ontario and a crisis was brewing. There was no longer any control over the issuance of badges. Anyone who wanted a badge could

FIGURE 10-1
Volunteer deputy conservation officers are valuable supporters of the conservation cause.

* 1.6 kilometres = 1 mile

get one and many who made requests were hunters and anglers with selfish motives. As a result, the badges became disrespectfully known as "cheap tin popcorn badges."

Accordingly, many C.O.s started to thin the deputies' ranks by initiating their own training regimens and by requiring that deputy conservation officers (D.C.O.s) work in direct partnership with them. Starting in 1979, the Minister of Natural Resources directly appointed all deputies and, the following year, they received a substantial metal badge worthy of the name. Tighter administrative control salvaged their reputation as altruistic volunteers.

Today there are 525 D.C.O.s across Ontario. Many are M.N.R. staff who donate their services during off-duty hours and many are "outside" volunteers hailing from all walks of life. Occasionally, deputies have been paid for short-term projects such as running creel censuses, administering public hunts and working as port observers to enforce commercial fishing regulations.

The deputy system—providing local support staff to detect violations, conduct resource management projects and collect vital information from the public—has acted increasingly as an unofficial training ground for fully fledged C.O.s. The system succeeds largely because of its community base. As Manitoulin C.O. Ian Anderson commented: "The deputy, unlike many C.O.s, is not an outsider imposing the will of the distant bureaucracy. People are more likely to give information to someone that they know."

The indomitable Felix (Phil) Fisher exemplifies the selflessness and devotion shown by many D.C.O.s. Born in 1906, he signed on as a deputy warden in 1930 and is still carrying a badge and working long hours for the sake of his beloved fish and wildlife.

Fisher's lifestyle imparts new meaning to the word "volunteer." While regularly employed, he assisted C.O.s—"damned good fellas, every one"—in the Niagara District where he has lived all his life. Since retiring from Cyanamid Inc. in 1971, Fisher has converted part of his house into an M.N.R. office, which is open seven days a week—from 8:00 a.m. to 8:00 p.m.—to keep the public informed on hunting and fishing matters. There, he issues hunting and fishing licences and export permits for bear, deer and moose, and he stamps or seals trappers' furs. Each year, between 1,500 and 1,800 people traipse through his makeshift office. "I have a home here," he acknowledged, "but much of the time you wouldn't think it's private at all."

For his untold hours of service, Fisher receives only a standard licence issuer's fee, a lifetime's commitment to con-

Starting in 1979, the Minister of Natural Resources directly appointed all deputies and, the following year, they received a substantial metal badge worthy of the name.

FIGURE 10-2
The indomitable Felix (Phil) Fisher (left) sells Ontario's first 1986 resident fish licence to then Minister of Natural Resources Vince Kerrio.

servation having brought him "not a cent." And that suits him just fine. "It's born in me," he said of his vocation. "I can't shake it."

In particular, Fisher has done much work with the local deer population, feeding them in the wild, assisting with biological research projects and bottle feeding fawns at home with the help of his wife, Doreen, and sons, Samuel and Philip. From 1945 to 1983, as a deputy C.O., he collected 400 roadkill deer, keeping a written record of each one.

Not that his relationship with the government has always been cosy. He had just applied for a full-time warden's job in 1934 when Mitchell Hepburn was elected premier and promptly fired many of the province's game wardens. The purge even cost Fisher his job as a deputy. But he kept volunteering and for several years teamed up, instead, with the O.P.P. and the R.C.M.P. After much cajoling and persuasion, he finally accepted the return of his deputy's badge and forty-one years later—in 1986—received an award from former Minister Vince Kerrio "in recognition of over fifty-five years of dedicated service."

* * * * *

There's an old saying that goes, "The finest conservation measures are not written in the statute books, but in the heart and conscience of the sportsman." Even before the first game wardens were appointed, sports enthusiasts from Ontario's founding clubs were calling for stern measures to ensure the survival of fish and game. Their contribution was acknowledged by Chief Warden Edwin Tinsley in 1898 when he noted that "numerous instances have been reported of [sports enthusiasts] prosecuting infractions brought to their notice, which augurs well for the future."

Rod and Gun in Canada magazine (launched in 1899) advocated a pro-conservation stance, an example followed by other sporting publications. Meanwhile, many rod and gun clubs were playing their part in pricking their members' consciences by drawing up their own laws within the new framework of legislation. After as many as 2,600 ducks had been taken by one gun in a season, the Long Point Club set an example in 1895 by making a by-law that no more than 500 ducks be shot on their reserve by any one member.

In 1899, S.T. Bastedo, deputy commissioner of the Ontario Fisheries Branch, urged the formation of more clubs and protective associations to aid the government in "the great work of protection." Nevertheless, to take a stand against poachers and all who would lay waste to the natural environment was often to invite retaliation.

Before the First World War, Oliver Adams, vice-president of the Ontario Forest, Fish and Game Protective Association, who demonstrated the importance of protecting game fish in the St. Lawrence River to the citizens of Gananoque and district, was warned by many people that his new summer home in the district would be burned down by "the lawless element." Sure enough, shortly after leaving his residence that first season, he learned that the property had been reduced to ashes.

Threats and intimidation constrained many who wished to act on behalf of fish, game and wildlife habitat. But the driving force of conservation would not be bullied into submission. Members of rod and gun clubs across the province placed themselves solidly in support of their local wardens by initiating projects ranging from fish stocking to planting hedgerows on farmland.

The St. Catharines and Lincoln County Game and Fish Protective Association, for example, handed out packages of evergreen tree seeds to gun licence issuers for distribution to all hunters, asking that they plant the seeds while ranging the fields and woods. Also, multi-flora rose plants from Holland were given freely to anyone willing to plant them along fence rows or on unused corners of farmland. The rose's thick-growing briars made excellent cover for game birds while the seed pods stood above the snow, providing winter feed.

Threats and intimidation constrained many who wished to act on behalf of fish, game and wildlife habitat.

Dating back to the 1920s, fish stocking was a popular community venture. The local warden would coordinate the arrival of consignments of hatchery fingerlings by train or fish truck with a rag-tag army of sports enthusiasts armed with an assortment of jars, buckets and tubs. Once the fish had been unloaded, the race was on to deposit them in designated lakes and rivers, the warden endeavouring to keep track of the number of fish and their destinations.

Until a permanent fish ladder was built in 1977, members of the Georgian Bay Hunters and Anglers Club worked with local C.O. Mike Thede to help struggling rainbow trout climb the C.P.R. concrete bridge foundation spanning the Sturgeon River in Simcoe County. They purchased and filled gabion baskets and dug out rocks below the dam to form jumping pools; they even built a wooden fish ladder. And every spring, they joined Thede in netting rainbows and lifting them over the dam.

The tiny township of Hagerman (pop. 400) in Parry Sound District has spent tens of thousands of dollars over the past fifty years hiring guardians to deter poaching on Whitestone Lake's pickerel spawning beds. In 1940, the township provided a truck, tank and people to reintroduce adult pickerel that had been live-trapped in Georgian Bay by the Department of Game and Fisheries. The guardians have since been protecting this initial investment.

The year 1926 saw the inaugural meeting of the Toronto Anglers Association, which became the Federation of Anglers and, in 1941, the Ontario Federation of Anglers and

FIGURE 10-3
C.O. Herb Clark, under the watchful eyes of local youngsters, stocks a lake with fish, an example for future generations.

Hunters (O.F.A.H.). Today the O.F.A.H. boasts 73,000 members and 470 affiliated clubs. For decades, the O.F.A.H. has been in the forefront of community action that supports, directly or indirectly, the work of conservation officers.

In 1957, when the Department of Lands and Forests introduced a compulsory hunter safety certificate course, club members were quick to cooperate in providing the necessary training. The Federation's Report-A-Poacher programme—involving the distribution of more than 200,000 violation cards—tells the public how to alert investigating officers when poaching is witnessed.

Citizens have rallied in a number of Ontario centres—among them, Espanola, Sudbury and Wawa—to support special programmes run in conjunction with Crime Stoppers International. Unsolved poaching incidents are graphically re-enacted on television and described on the radio and in the local newspapers in hope of reaching people who can lead C.O.s to the culprits. Anonymous callers who provide information resulting in convictions are rewarded with cash prizes.

Timmins was the first city to launch the programme in September, 1989. Dramatically, the very first call led to the swift arrest of two men who had illegally slaughtered a moose. As soon as the tip came in, C.O.s drove to a city house, arrested and took statements from two men in possession of the dead animal, and returned to the office—all within eighty minutes. "This is an excellent programme," enthused Timmins C.O. Jim Abbott. "There's a lot of potential for expansion."

By 1991, Ministry involvement in the Crime Stoppers program had expanded to three other areas—Sault Ste. Marie/Algoma, Kenora and Niagara Falls. Then on November 8, 1991, Bud Wildman, Minister of Natural Resources, announced that the Ministry was expanding its involvement in Crime Stoppers. As part of his announcement, the Minister appointed Dave Ferguson, Enforcement Specialist in Sudbury, as the Minister's first Provincial Coordinator for the Crime Stoppers program. He further stated that a liaison officer would be appointed in each Ministry district.

Since 1984, the O.F.A.H. has pioneered, with the assistance of ministry staff including C.O.s, the reintroduction of wild turkeys in Ontario. (The current wild turkey population of 10,000 has grown from the 276 birds released between 1984 and 1987.) The federation holds two six-day junior conservation schools each July and more than 250,000 young people have seen a conservation education slide show explaining urban encroachment, habitat loss, and what can be done to ensure healthy populations of wildlife.

Conservation officers have also been involved in many educational projects over the years. These, in turn, have led to a public appreciation of C.O.s' protective role and, in many cases, practical contributions.

Education often starts with entertainment. In 1921, the Department of Game and Fisheries staged its first public exhibit at the Canadian National Exhibition featuring several live animals that drew the public into more instructional features such as forest fire prevention and gun safety. Since 1948, C.O.s have maintained a strong presence at the ministry exhibit at the Toronto Sportsmen's Show as well as many other fairs and exhibitions throughout the province.

Since 1985, C.O.s have played a role in Project WILD, which has instructed over 17,000 teachers in wildlife education so that the message of conservation can be passed on to the younger generation. National Wildlife Week in April sees many C.O.s giving talks and workshops in school classrooms across the province. And the ministry's Community Fisheries Involvement Program (C.F.I.P.) and Community Wildlife Involvement Program (C.W.I.P.) invite schoolchildren along with other groups in the community to participate in projects designed to maintain and rehabilitate natural resources.

When Wingham C.O. Ken Maronets received a call from teacher Bill

FIGURE 10-4
An investment in future abundance. C.O. Doug Marshall (left) presents members of the Muskoka Lakes Association with a bag of young trees for planting along cottage shorelines in Port Carling.

Raynard enquiring about the C.W.I.P., little did he realize that enthusiasm for conservation projects would soon be spreading from school to school in the district.

In 1988, Maronets led the students at Raynard's public school—Howick Central in Huron County—in removing a beaver dam from a nearby stream. The following year, he encouraged the students to develop a hedgerow between a wetland and an upland area. More projects followed at other schools and, as they were successfully accomplished, Maronets received more and more requests for his services from schools throughout the district. "First, there's a spark of interest," he said. "The next thing you know, you've got a raging fire."

C.O.s act as advisers and liaison officers in many C.F.I.P. and C.W.I.P. activities, which provide funds so that schools, fish and game clubs, aboriginal groups, cottagers' associations, naturalists' groups, lodge owners and tourist operators can conduct projects of their own making.

When C.O. Pat Brown was assigned in the spring of 1985 to work with a group of residents and tourist operators on a C.F.I.P. project to build a pickerel jar hatchery in Holdridge Creek, near Marten River, he had his doubts about community involvement. Those doubts evaporated the night he arrived on the job.

"I was very impressed with the turn-out and the way people were pitching in without being paid a nickel to be there," he said. "A number of people stayed on until well after 1:00 a.m.—and it was a week night." What impressed, and surprised, Brown even more was that one or two of the hatchery builders—were known to have a history of poaching!

First Nation people have often taken the initiative to preserve a faltering natural resource. In the late 1940s, when the registered trapline system was being implemented, the Ojibwas of Ogoki on the Albany River petitioned the Fish and Wildlife Branch to set aside part of their hunting grounds as a pine marten preserve. The marten was then extremely scarce throughout northern Ontario and excessive trapping threatened the animal with extinction. Judicious management—which included the Ogoki marten preserve—enabled marten to rebound to their former abundance over the next twenty years.

More recently, in 1988, Leonard Dokis, former chief of the Dokis First Nation straddling the French River, approached the M.N.R. in a bid to undertake C.F.I.P. projects on the reserve. The projects—to improve walleye spawning beds and build an eight-jar hatchery and rearing pond—have been a great success and have helped to instill "a really strong sense of stewardship towards the resource," said Roger Wolfe, fish and wildlife supervisor at North Bay.

Although the rearing pond was hit hard by a storm in the spring of 1990, three lakes on the reserve had already been stocked. "The programme seems to be catching on," said Dokis, who runs a camp and marina on the French River. "It's a good start." Similarly, tourist resort operator Ray Holl of Pointe au Baril heads a volunteer group that annually rears pickerel fingerlings for release in Georgian Bay.

For as long as there have been game wardens, trappers across northern Ontario have acted unofficially as extra pairs of eyes and ears for the officers. In the *Globe and Mail* of November 25, 1939, D.J. Taylor, Deputy Minister of Game and Fisheries, said: "The trapper becomes a conservationist in his own right. He is a game warden himself and protects his own area." Commented Bill Russell, president of the 3,000-member Ontario Trappers Association and a trapper of forty-three years' standing: "If there are any problems on the traplines—perhaps the beaver population starts to decline or if a moose or a deer has been harvested illegally—trappers will contact a conservation officer right away."

While working alongside C.O.s in trapper education and fur management courses, trappers have also been involved in a variety of conservation projects—from planting red and white clover as feed for birds and rabbits to converting marten box traps into bird houses during the closed season. "We see C.O.s as our very close friends," said Russell, who stressed that the more management work is undertaken, the more fur-bearing animals there will be. "We are all working towards the same goals and that is why our relationship is one of ongoing cooperation."

> "If there are any problems on the traplines—perhaps the beaver population starts to decline—or if a moose or a deer has been harvested illegally—trappers will contact a conservation officer right away."

Just as trappers keep their eyes peeled in the bush, so do the people who run tourist lodges in northern Ontario. Any number of sightings might be reason to call in the local C.O.: a forest fire, the dumping of garbage on Crown land, illegal fishing or a rash of poaching activity.

Lloyd Lindner, who runs Camp Hiawatha on the north shore of Lake Huron, contacted the Espanola detachment some years ago after stumbling upon a hunting party, a pack of dogs and a deer that had been shot out-of-season. Although the hunters laughed at Lindner's challenge, the C.O.s' rapid response to his call ensured they were apprehended.

"We have an excellent relationship, a family relationship, with conservation officers," said Lindner, who is also past president of the Northern Ontario Tourist Outfitters Association (N.O.T.O.), which represents 850 proprietors. "Their job is to protect the resource and we want to do the same."

The Federation of Ontario Naturalists, which celebrated its sixtieth anniversary in 1991, considers C.O.s "very valuable allies" in their battle against environmental degradation and expects its 30,000 members to be vigilant in the field, reporting any infractions or violations. "C.O.s deserve all the respect they can get and more," declared president Mary Smith. "I'm glad that they are there—but I think we need more of them."

C.O.s have also worked very closely with park wardens assigned to Ontario's provincial parks. Park wardens, introduced in 1976, wear a light brown uniform with a peaked cap, often carry handcuffs and batons and are paid for their services. Each summer, more than 400 of them are on duty across the province.

Like C.O.s, park wardens have the authority of an O.P.P. constable within provincial park boundaries. While C.O.s are frequently on hand during peak holiday periods, park wardens generally keep the peace unaided. The force is largely made up of students aspiring to work in security and law enforcement.

Said Jim Moore, a former C.O. who has been a park warden for the past eleven years, "wardens are like police officers in the parks." Having retired as Dryden's fish and wildlife supervisor in 1979 to take up sheep farming, Moore works summers as enforcement coordinator at Sandbanks and North Beach provincial parks in Prince Edward County where he supervises seven park wardens and four security officers. In an average summer, more than 350,000 people visit these parks and more than 600 charges—mainly for liquor offences, rowdyism and vandalism—are laid.

Sometimes, C.O.s find their backing comes from unorthodox sources. In April, 1979, C.O. Brett Hodsdon was called to Port Hope after four self-styled vigilantes had spotted two men netting rainbow trout in the Ganaraska River during the closed season. The citizens moved in, a chase ensued and

> **In an average summer, more than 350,000 people visit these parks and more than 600 charges—mainly for liquor offences, rowdyism and vandalism—are laid.**

FIGURE 10-5
Park Wardens, introduced into provincial parks in 1976, are like police officers in the parks. They work very closely with conservation officers.

one of the poachers was captured after a scuffle. The other poacher was later taken into police custody and both men were subsequently convicted.

Whatever their personal or political motivation, helping hands are invaluable and C.O.s will gladly accept all the public assistance that comes their way. It can be said without exaggeration that C.O.s draw their professional lifeblood from a willing, supportive public. A century of experience has shown that active cooperation is not only a boon to enforcement and resource management, but also a wise investment in some priceless assets: the land, waters, fish and wildlife of Ontario.

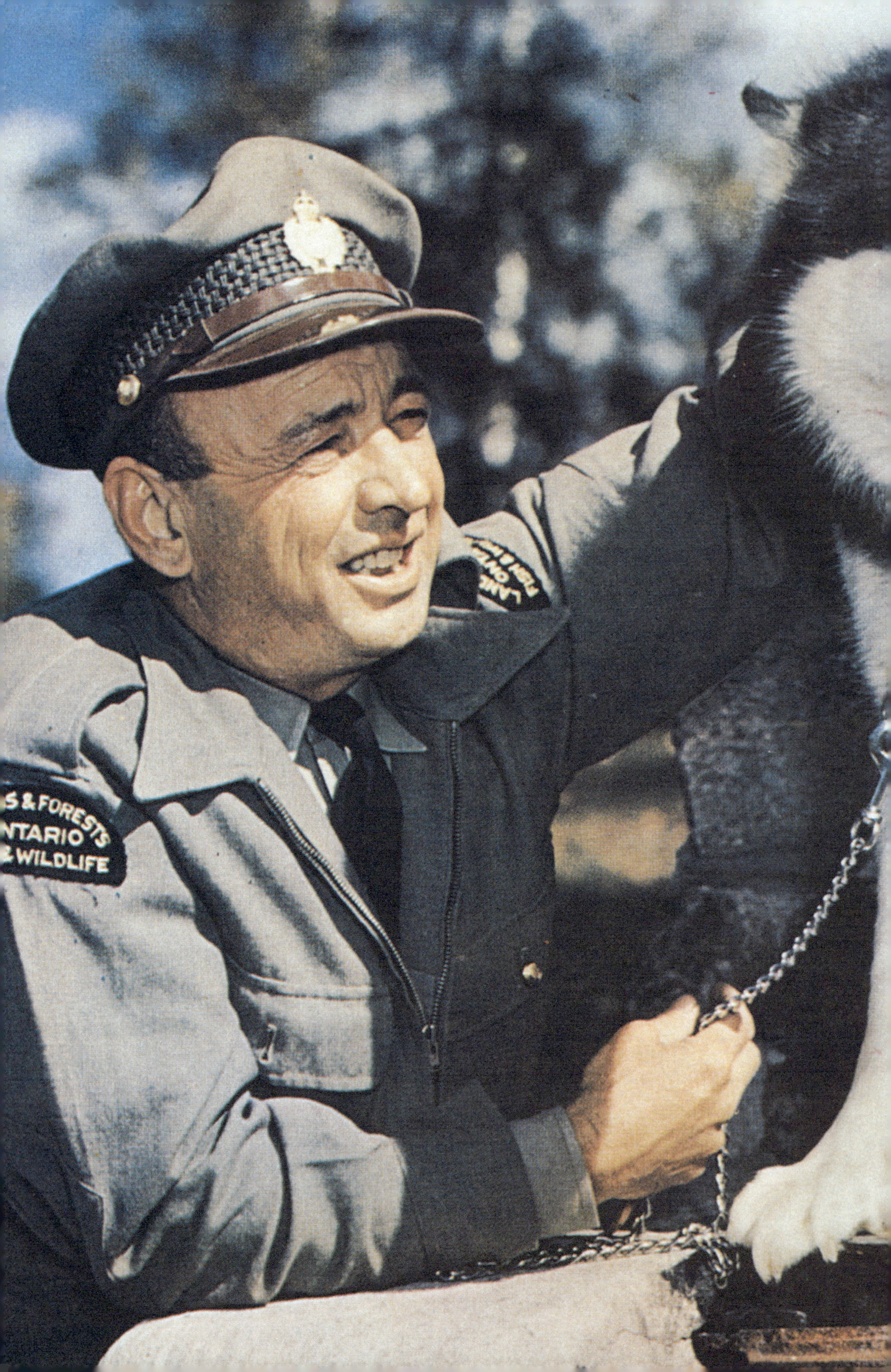
S & FORESTS
NTARIO
WILDLIFE

Chapter Eleven: Four-Legged Deputies

The Canadian game warden of yesteryear is a legendary figure. Bundled up like some veritable "Ben Hur of the Arctic," he is often portrayed standing astride a sled yelling "Mush!" to a team of powerful huskies dashing headlong into windblown snow. This characterization is actually closer to the truth than might be expected. A conservation officer was severely restricted without a dog team in the wintertime. Snowshoes, though useful, could take one only so far, so fast. Nevertheless, there was one drawback to constant canine accompaniment: because sleigh dogs were inclined to howl at the moon or echo the cries of wolves, poachers would sometimes get wind that the warden was on his way.

The last warden to patrol regularly on the back of a sleigh was Len Cote, remembered by many as "the dog mushing conservation officer from Marten River." Cote, who died in 1989 at the age of seventy-eight, would make the rounds of Nipissing Crown Game Preserve in the 1950s with the help of a team of Siberian huskies. He loved his dogs—particularly a lead dog called Smokey.

"Honest, unpretentious and tough when he needed to be, Len was a real softie when it came to dogs," said Mike Buss, M.N.R. biologist and a long-time friend of the officer. "As he was a bachelor, his dogs were his family and came before anything else."

Breaking trail in deep, fresh snow, Cote—the son of warden Bill Cote—would stride ahead of the huskies on the outward journey, relishing the thrill of being able to ride over a packed trail on the

LEFT: *C.O. Len Cote—the last warden to patrol regularly on the back of a sleigh—and his favourite husky, "Smokey," at Marten River in the 1950s.*

return trip. Out on patrol for several days at a time, he would make overnight stops at cabins in the preserve.

Retired C.O. Carl Monk remembers leaving one of these cabins in company with Cote one spring morning just as the ice was beginning to lift along the shoreline of a nearby lake. Undeterred by the softening conditions, Cote drove his dogs out across the lake, leaving a coal-oil lantern burning in a tree beside the cabin. "When we returned that evening we hit the lake as it was beginning to get dark," Monk recalled. "The dogs could see the light of the lantern and they became excited, knowing they were almost home. Len and I, meanwhile, became aware that a stretch of water—about eight feet* wide—had opened up against the shore. Len was yelling at the dogs to stop, but those dogs had a lot of power and they just wanted to get home. I jumped off onto the ice but Len stayed aboard for a good soaking as the dogs charged right through the water and onto the land."

On more obedient days, Cote's huskies would haul blocks of ice to supply fire rangers' ice houses where provisions would be stored throughout the long, hot summers. Sometimes, when a battery-dead truck refused to start, the huskies would be hooked up to pull the vehicle until its engine turned over. In appreciation of the dogs' efforts, the Department of Lands and Forests paid for their food.

Cote placed his working team on the racing circuit, competing successfully in Quebec and various U.S. states as well as in winter carnivals closer to home at places such as Temagami, Kirkland Lake and North Bay. By 1967, Cote had more than sixty dogs, an extended family he fed and watered with tireless affection. Sadly, however, his beloved Smokey was killed by a bolt of lightning that rushed down a pole and along the dog's steel chain.

FIGURE 11-1
A "dog mushing" C.O. Al Pozzo is pictured with his team of Siberian huskies near the wilderness outpost of Franz in 1954.

* 30 centimetres = 1 foot

Another "dog mushing" C.O. was Al Pozzo, who drove his team of Siberian huskies through the wilds of the Chapleau Crown Game Preserve between 1954 and 1957 while stationed in the wilderness outpost of Franz. Until the early 1960s, the White River District was accessible only by air and rail, and a dog team was essential.

Pozzo and his dogs, it is said, would take pleasure in turning themselves into a welcoming committee for tourists, granting alighting passengers from incoming trains an authentic glimpse of the northland. The Algoma Central Railway granted Pozzo special permission to ride the swath it had cut through the forest so that he could pick up moose and deer that might have been hit by trains. Habitually, he would load his dogs and sleigh on a baggage car, travelling down the track as far as he wished before unloading his canine cargo and charging into the bush.

Pozzo's son, John Pozzo, told of being raised in a department house with sled dogs ("they were like family pets") yapping in the backyard and the perpetual anticipation of sleigh rides. His father, he said, was known to remark on the advent of snow machines, as snowmobiles were first called: "I prefer the dog team because dogs are far more reliable. They don't break down and leave me far from home."

Pozzo is well remembered by ninety-year-old Aubrey Dunne, of Huntsville, who, as district forester at White River, was his boss for several years. Dunne worked as a ranger in Algonquin Park during the 1930s and regularly used a dogsled to transport building materials for log cabins as well as to scout relentlessly for poachers' tracks. In good travelling conditions on packed snow, Dunne would travel eighty kilometres in a day with his dogs—a yelping assortment of huskies and mongrels. "Those dogs were a real help to me," he said. "Having a good lead dog was the key to the whole set-up."

On long patrols, Dunne would carry ten days' supply of food for the dogs as well as for himself. The dogs' staple diet was corn meal and beef tallow, which Dunne would stir into boiling water during overnight stops. "It was a pretty rugged life," Dunne allowed, "but a healthy one."

Northern life outdoors in wintry weather was rugged all right. So horribly cold were the conditions encountered by overseer Andy Gagnon and his dog team during the 1940s that one of his huskies froze to death and another was severely frostbitten! Gagnon, a former trapper, would drive his dogs north from Moosonee along the coastline of James Bay, where wind-chilled temperatures can plummet to minus sixty-two degrees Celsius in mid-winter. Pausing at scattered aboriginal communities, he would register traplines, seal fur, and issue trapping licences and quotas for various species.

In 1950, a mongrel belonging to C.O. Sam Nodwell paid the supreme sacrifice after hauling provisions for officers trudging through Gogama's icy hinterland. "Two officers had been flown out to inspect traplines with two dogs and a toboggan," said Nodwell, who was fish and wildlife supervisor in Gogama at the time. "When a Beaver aircraft on skis arrived to pick them up, one of the dogs—my dog—raced up to the plane before the engine stopped idling. He always liked to get into the aircraft, knowing that he wouldn't have to pull the toboggan any more. But this time he ran into the propeller, which cut off his head."

These dogs are more likely to ride in upholstered vehicles than pull a sleigh, but their dedication and usefulness endure.

The original four-legged deputies were horses, the preferred mode of transport for wardens unable to reach their destinations by train. As recently as the 1950s, hired steeds were pressed into service to drag the carcasses of big game from the bush. But horses were ungainly animals for heavily wooded terrain and, besides, they ran the risk of being mistaken by over-zealous hunters for more edible targets, such as moose and deer. Whenever C.O.s rode horses into the woods they would string bells on their bridles in hope of keeping reckless riflemen at bay.

With the imminent passing of the dog sleigh era, certain breeds of dogs—usually German shepherds and Labradors—were adopted more and more by C.O.s as companions, protectors and trackers of poachers and poaching evidence. These dogs are more likely to ride in upholstered vehicles than pull a sleigh, but their dedication and usefulness endure.

Official recognition of canine prowess came in 1953 when Tor—a Great Dane that ranged Toronto's Don Valley in search of poachers—was appointed an honorary deputy game warden, complete with badge, by the Deputy Minister of Lands and Forests. A full-page picture of Tor ran in the magazine *Sylva*, showing him surrounded by an array of rifles confiscated from violators the Great Dane had helped to apprehend.

Carl Monk's Weimaraner hunting dog named Queenie Von Franz often proved her worth during the late 1950s. Her assistance was never more gratifying than the morning Monk, while checking two duck hunters on the west arm of Lake Nipissing, counted sixteen ringneck ducks—their full quota—lying in the shallows. The limit in those days was eight ducks per person and the hunters denied shooting more than the law allowed.

"As we were chatting," said Monk, "Queenie was patrolling the surrounding area and she began to find more ducks. She kept coming and going and, before long, had piled another sixteen ducks at my feet." The hunters, whose consternation can only be imagined, were later fined $70 each after being convicted of shooting more than their lawful limit.

In the 1960s, C.O. Peter Nunan became known locally in Thunder Bay as "the man with the black dog" because he was virtually inseparable from

Buck, his black Labrador.

"I would take Buck with me everywhere," said Nunan, who retired as regional enforcement specialist in 1989. "He would follow the trail of anything you wanted, from a man to a moose. If ice fishermen tried to hide illegal catches under the snow, Buck would dig them out. On countless occasions, he led me to where ducks or deer or moose had been buried."

When Nunan carried his canoe over portages and couldn't see what was ahead, Buck would direct his master by leading the way. He would ride behind Nunan on his snowmobile and sit in Nunan's truck with his paws resting on the back of the driver's seat, his head on Nunan's shoulder. Whenever duty required that Nunan sleep overnight in his vehicle, Buck would lie beside him.

"Buck never seemed to sleep," said Nunan. "If I was snoozing in the truck and a vehicle was approaching from a long way off, the dog would always hear it well in advance and give a little "ruff!" to wake me up. He was strictly a one-man dog and didn't care much for anyone else. I never had to lock the truck—he was all teeth and claws if anyone tried to get in!"

When it came to following a scent, few dogs could emulate the unswerving nose of Nero, a thirty-eight-kilogram black-and-tan bloodhound owned by C.O. Dave Kenney.

When it came to following a scent, few dogs could emulate the unswerving nose of Nero, a thirty-eight-kilogram black-and-tan bloodhound owned by C.O. Dave Kenney. Kenney acquired the dog in 1979 with the intent of using him for tracking hunters and anglers suspected of violations. Nero adapted brilliantly to his role and helped to solve many fish and wildlife cases for his handler. But there was more work in store for the officer's dog.

Nero's abilities were soon noticed by the police force in Espanola where Kenney was stationed from 1976 to 1982. The bloodhound was used to track criminals, and he is credited with putting several criminals behind bars. When just a pup of six months, Nero bounded happily in pursuit of a police suspect after sniffing human scent on a cardboard box that had been disturbed in a night warehouse break-in. Darkness notwithstanding, Nero's nose went straight to a bush where a seventeen-year-old youth readily surrendered to police. On another occasion, he aided the O.P.P. in finding a Sudbury woman who was lost in cedar swamps near Silver Water on Manitoulin Island.

Most of the time, however, the lovably awkward bloodhound was the C.O's helpmate. "Nero was an amazing animal, exceptional even for his breed," said Kenney of the dog, which died in 1988. "Every day I would take him with me on patrol and most days he would find something of value, whether it was a cluster of fishing lines, a spear or a gun hidden in the grass [or] slaughtered game... A good dog like Nero provides a C.O. with the most valuable assistance."

The accompanying presence of a dog has helped many an officer confronted with a threatening situation. C.O. Gord Black recalled the night in 1969 he faced four drunkenly aggressive hunters 140 kilometres from his Gogama detachment office. "There was no radio contact in those days," said Black. "We were in the middle of nowhere and these guys were going to clean my clock."

"I said: 'Back off, fellas, I've got a dog' and walked back to my truck and opened the door. Rip, a pet Siberian husky that Len Cote had given me, trotted out and sat beside me. He had a wide space between his eyes and he looked vicious. They didn't know it, but Rip was so friendly he might very well have licked them to death!" The mere sight of the dog inspired sufficient apprehension to relieve the threat of violence.

When C.O. Ron Hartford was assaulted by drunken anglers in 1984, only the snarling of Midnight—his German shepherd restrained in the ministry truck—prevented his attackers from doing more harm. Said Hartford's

FIGURE 11-2
C.O. Brian Morrison and his black Labrador retriever, Shadow, are the first tracking team to be trained at the Ontario Provincial Polices's canine unit in Brampton. Brian and Shadow began their one-year trial in January 1991.

wife, Judy: "Our dog earned her food for the rest of her life that day."

While C.O.s in Nova Scotia, New Brunswick and many U.S. states have long been assisted by all-purpose canine units, Ontario's M.N.R. has yet to support this use of dogs. C.O. Brian Morrison set out to change this situation by proposing a trial canine programme he hoped would demonstrate dogs' effectiveness in enforcement work.

In January, 1991, Morrison and a black Labrador named Shadow began a one-year trial and were soon travelling across northeastern Ontario.

Shadow—"a real clown," according to Morrison—is particularly adept at tracking and detection and the dog's mere presence deters would-be violators. Said Morrison: "Casting back and forth, Shadow will find a hat, a knife, articles of clothing, concealed fish and deer meat, anything that may be stashed, hidden or thrown away. Also, because people tend to have a Rin Tin Tin idea of dogs fighting evil, Shadow works well in public relations presentations to schools and colleges. Kids love the dog."

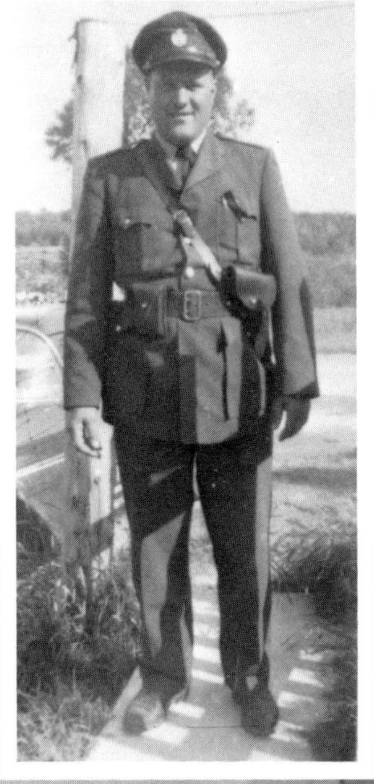
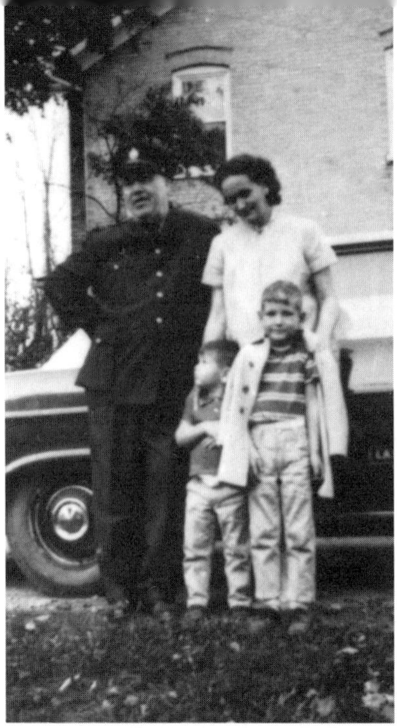
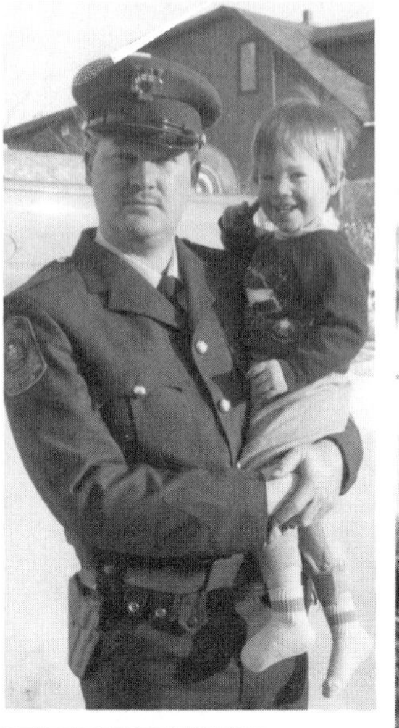
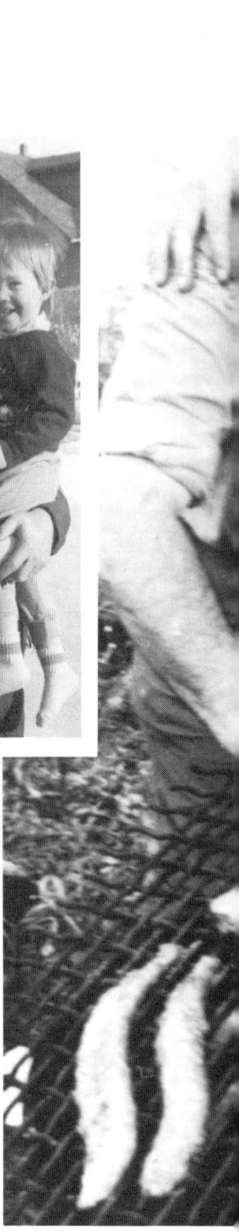
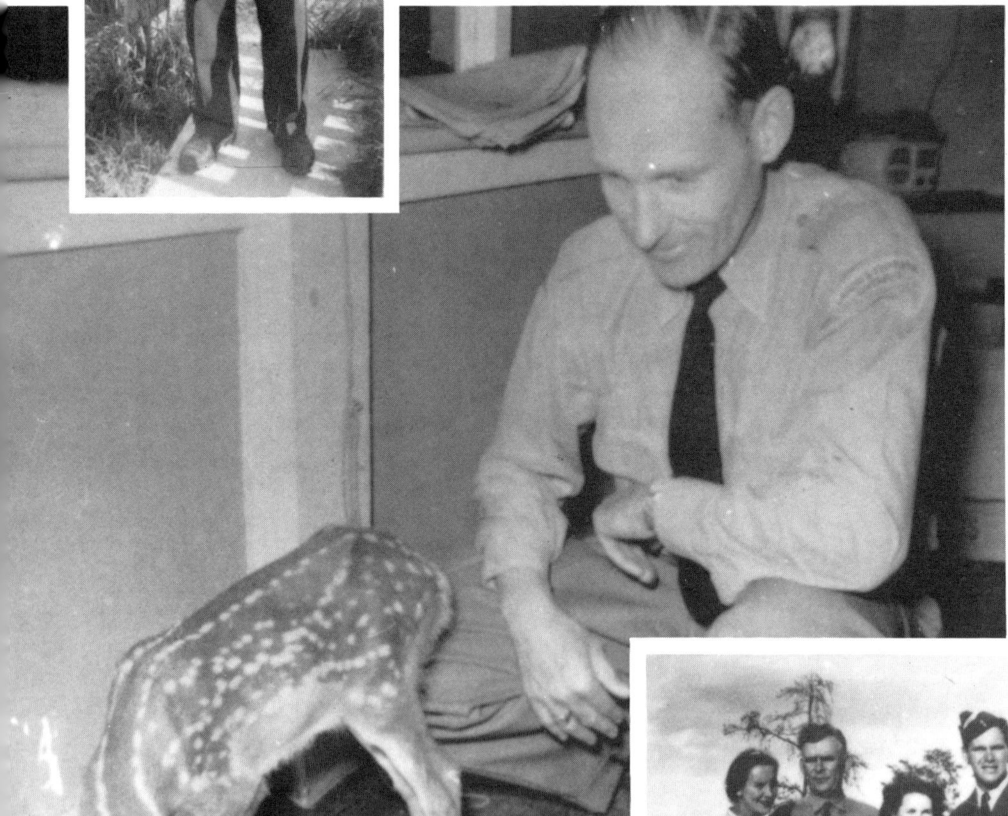
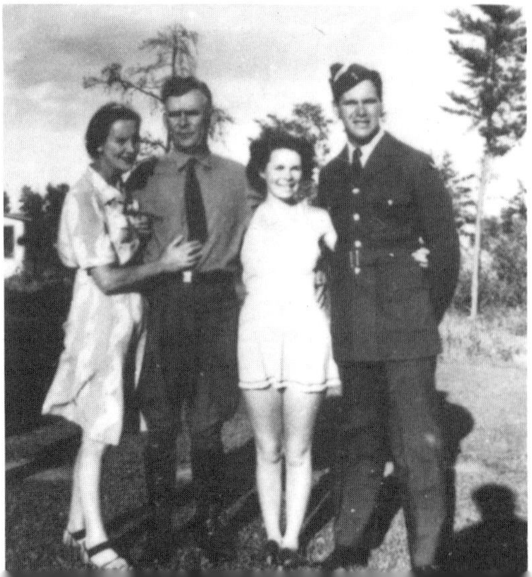

Chapter Twelve: The Home Front

Christmas morning was only hours away and C.O. Ken Snowden had managed to book off work long enough to do some last-minute gift shopping with his family. With his wife, Linda, and three young daughters, Snowden was about to leave home for the nearest mall. Then the telephone rang. On the line was someone from Maple District Office telling him that a pair of hikers had found the shot and gutted carcass of a deer covered with branches at the Caledon reserve of the Ontario Federation of Naturalists.

"Can't you wait until we get the shopping done and then go?" pleaded Linda. But her husband, knowing time was at a premium, quickly made his apologies and rushed to the scene with fellow officer Brad Labadie. There, after a chase, Snowden charged two men with unlawfully hunting deer.

For thirty-four-year-old Snowden, the incident was the highlight of his three-year career as a C.O., even though it meant the disruption of his family's Christmas Eve. After processing charges and disposing of the deer, he managed to return home around 7:00 p.m., just when Amanda, six, Kelly, three, and nine-month-old Katlin were getting ready for bed. By the time he had finished writing up his notes ninety minutes later, the kids were asleep.

"We *had* plans for Christmas Eve," said Snowden ruefully. "You know, to have a fire,

LEFT: *Homefront scenes contributed by staff and friends.*

Christmas stories and to go for a walk to look at the lights. But, well, that's the nature of the job."

Added Linda: "You learn to live with it and let it go."

In some respects, nothing has changed for conservation officers in 100 years. When duty calls, a C.O. must kiss domestic obligations goodbye and follow the trail. The "nature of the job" was always thus, making the home front every bit as challenging as the larger world outside. Since the earliest days, intense working demands and pressures have taken a heavy toll on domestic contentment. Constant professional commitment—a standard trait among C.O.s—can exact a price of displeasure and even divorce back home. Although no statistics have been compiled for marriage break-ups within the ranks, divorces are known to be disturbingly commonplace.

> **When duty calls, a C.O. must kiss domestic obligations goodbye and follow the trail.**

Back in 1900, Dr. G. A. MacCallum, chair of the Board of Game Commissioners, spoke of game wardens as having "greater territories than they can possibly look after," adding that it was "absurd" to expect one person to police hundreds of square miles of woods. Absurd or not, the job had to be done, and spouses often spent weeks waiting, wondering and praying.

In their husbands' absence, the wives shouldered the burden of wardens' work that had been left behind. They were often presented at the door with injured, sickly and sometimes even rabid animals; and also were expected to provide hunting and fishing information on demand.

Even after a forty-hour week was introduced in the late 1950s, wives and girlfriends were still wondering whether the burdensome workload would ever make room for the home and hearth. Overtime pay—introduced gradually in the 1960s and 1970s—was authorized so sparsely that, as late as 1985, most C.O.s were putting in well over 100 hours of "free" overtime a year. Some officers regularly logged more than 300 unpaid hours annually.

In 1968, Bob Record, president of the Peterborough Fish and Game Association and a long-time deputy C.O., wrote an open letter to his club members lamenting the impossible situation faced by local C.O. Johnny McCulloch. While the city had a police force of over 200 officers to safeguard streets, buildings and highways, Peterborough's lone C.O. was required to patrol seven townships. A similar dilemma confronted every enforcer. The letter went on: "Our local conservation officer must patrol fields, lakes and highways, run a telephone service and complaint department 24 hours a day, run hunter training examinations, seal furs, issue licences, run a creel census, be his own secretary, send in reports to Lindsay as well as try to be a husband and father and public relations man in the community. I wonder what he does in his spare time?"

Just the notion of "spare time" brings a chuckle to the lips of old-time C.O.s. They will tell you how hunting and fishing seasons have dictated their absence from a succession of family celebrations—especially weddings and birthday parties. They will tell you of being late for supper on countless occasions and being beset by telephone calls at all hours of the day and night. But they will also tell you they loved the job, the outdoors, the independence and the endless variety of tasks. When people showed up at the door carrying injured animals, sure, they'd take them in. Or their wives would.

Veteran officer Gord Black brought home a host of creatures ranging from hawks and owls to bear cubs, deer and, once, a loose-boweled moose calf. An injured loon commandeered the Blacks' bathtub for three weeks and an "old squaw" duck, wounded by hunters, sat in a cardboard box watching television incessantly. Black, who said that his eight children received a wildlife education by partaking in the ongoing drama, even gave physical therapy to a misshapen groundhog, which eventually waddled away.

FIGURE 12-1
C.O. Gord Black gives bear cubs food and shelter in the spring of 1981.

Peter Skuce remembered his father, C.O. Ed Skuce, caring for injured birds, fawns, bear cubs and a large bald eagle. "We were living at Pembroke when I went out with my father to release the eagle," said Skuce. "I was nine or ten years old at the time and I remember those big wings unfolding as the bird flew away—quite a thrill." Of his childhood as a C.O.'s son, Skuce added: "There wasn't a lot of money. It was a spartan kind of existence. But I will always remember the respect in the home for the environment—being a game warden was more than just a job for father."

Being a warden was never merely an occupation; it was a way of life. In remote communities, especially, ministry personnel such as the C.O.s, *were* the government, the authority figure, the community counsellor and go-between, the kindly person that youngsters would go to for advice or who would drive you to hospital and pick up your medicine in an emergency. The C.O. was a police officer, a social worker, a nurse. Oh yes, and a game warden, too.

Before C.O.s were progressively installed in district offices during the 1960s, they worked out of their homes, a condition that was hardly conducive to domestic bliss. Not only was the C.O.'s wife expected to serve as an unpaid secretary, but also the home was likely to become a "warehouse" for all manner of equipment seized from hunters and anglers.

In 1969, the basement belonging to Cambridge C.O. Dale Gartley contained sixty-eight weapons, mostly shotguns and rifles, held in readiness for upcoming court hearings. Also in storage were traps, snares, snagging equipment and lunch buckets. "I wanted to go away for a week's holiday and so I called Preston police to tell them about having all these weapons in the house," said Gartley. "They were amazed to hear of such a thing and placed twenty-four-hour surveillance on the place until I returned!"

Over the past century, several sons have followed in their fathers' footsteps as game wardens. There are currently two father and son C.O. pairings in the province—Ken and Rick Maw and Terry and Mike

Humberstone. Moosonee's Terry Humberstone, who has spent more than thirty years as a C.O., said that he tried to dissuade his son, Mike, from following his professional example. "Not because I didn't want him to become a C.O.," he explained, "but because it's so difficult to land a full-time job and I didn't want to see my son go from contract to contract year after year while waiting to be accepted." But that's just what Mike did for seven years before landing a C.O.'s job at Red Lake. Added Terry: "I was probably as happy as he was to find out that he'd clicked as a candidate."

Ken Maw, a twenty-six-year veteran, believes that his son, Rick, got bitten by the conservation officer bug by watching him work out of their home at Burk's Falls from 1968 to 1978. Rick also watched his mother, Janet, work. Each fall, Janet issued up to 200 moose hunting licences a day from their home. "The knocks on the door would start at 6:00 a.m.," recalled Rick, who is based at Geraldton. "We put up a sign saying we were open from 8 until 5 but nobody paid much attention."

> "I'm surprised Rick did become a C.O. because I used to work enormous hours and hardly ever spent much time with the family."

"I'm surprised Rick did become a C.O. because I used to work enormous hours and hardly ever spent much time with the family," said Ken. "But a lot of work was done in the house around the table, coffee was always on, and other C.O.s and the public were always dropping in. And there were so many neat things going on to intrigue young children—like me bringing critters home."

"School counsellors tried to sway me towards degree programmes," added Rick. "But I kept coming back to the C.O.'s job because I wanted to work to protect the future of the resource." Donny Maw is the third conservation officer in the family. Stationed at Red Lake in 1982, he is Ken's nephew and Rick's cousin.

FIGURE 12-2
All in the family. From left, the three C.O.s named Maw serving in 1992—Nephew, Donny of Red Lake, Ken, of Dryden, and his son, Rick of Geraldton.

Two teams of brothers are among the C.O.s' ranks—Ernie and Andy Heerschap, and Rick and Mike Ladouceur.

The most disconcerting aspect of family life has always been the nagging fear that, because the C.O. is always on the front lines, something tragic may happen somewhere, somehow. But a warden's home, too, is not beyond the reach of lawbreakers who are determined to get even. Anticipating trouble after C.O. Ian Anderson relinquished his undercover role with Operation Rainbow Country in January, 1990, the M.N.R. installed a full security system with motion detectors in every room of his Manitoulin Island home.

When Donna Fry was a little girl, her family was always worried that her father Mel Miller, a C.O. from 1962 to 1989, might plunge through ice into a lake or get caught in a raging blizzard. But times and conditions have changed. Since being married to C.O. Jim Fry, Donna's anxiety has centred more on the possibility of her husband being attacked by criminals with high-powered weapons.

Back in 1981/82, Jim Fry investigated and charged some hard-core poachers in the Lake Simcoe area. The poachers responded by threatening the lives of Fry and his wife, slashing the tires of Fry's patrol car and throwing rocks at their house. Even Donna Fry's employer at the time, a doctor, would receive calls announcing that Fry would be killed.

The poachers responded by threatening the lives of Fry and his wife, slashing the tires of Fry's patrol car and throwing rocks at their house.

"My nerves were pretty well shot there for a while," said Fry. "If I had had kids at the time, I would either have put in for a compassionate move or this experience would have finished the marriage." While the tension eased in time, Fry's responsibilities continue and, as a precautionary measure, he has since purchased a Rottweiler as a family guard dog.

"The hardest of all," said Donna Fry, "is when Jim works undercover. I don't know where he is or what he is doing and, because he doesn't want me to worry, I'm usually kept in the dark until it's all over."

After C.O. Brett Hodsdon charged a pair of poachers for deer poaching in 1979, he and his wife, Wenda, were subjected to a string of reprisals that turned their home life in Emily township into a prolonged nightmare. A week into the investigation, Hodsdon's M.N.R. cruiser and Wenda's Honda were raked with bullets while parked in their driveway. Also, gasoline was poured over the cruiser's tires in an unsuccessful attempt to set the vehicle on fire.

In successive closed seasons, pickerel remains were dumped on their doorstep. One morning, after Wenda found that her car was not running properly, a mechanic informed her that the car's electrical wires had been deliberately cut. Their home was burgled, and Hodsdon's badge was stolen. When another poaching incident brought a further confrontation between Hodsdon and the pair, one of the two told him: "You know what

FIGURE 12-3
C.O. Ian Anderson pays high tribute to his wife Pat, who, like spouses of other C.O.s, must cope with the irregularities of her husband's work life. The couple live on Manitoulin Island with their two children, Ryan (left) and Erik.

happens when you start bothering us." He then made a string of death threats.

That was as much as Hodsdon could bear. "The day after the threats, I listed the house for sale," he said. "The main reason was concern for my wife. I didn't like to think of her being alone there."

Children can suffer, too. After C.O. Bill Tye seized gill nets from Lake Huron, his children—Stephanie, thirteen years old, and Dan, ten—were harassed and beaten up repeatedly by children at school. More intimidation followed. Tye heard from the O.P.P. that there was a contract to kill him, the tires of his cruiser were slashed and dead fish were left on the doorstep of their home.

The M.N.R. paid for his wife, Susan, and the two children to get away for a few days and, that weekend, Tye sat at home expecting the worst with a twelve-gauge shotgun across his knee and his German shepherd dog at the ready. Shortly afterwards, he applied for a transfer. "It really irked me that I had to leave," he said. "It was a very upsetting time for all of us."

So many are the headaches and heartaches that a C.O.'s wife must endure that C.O. Ian Anderson published a tribute to their patience in the winter, 1987, edition of the Ontario Conservation Officer's Association newsletter. His tribute concluded: "Who...would marry a warden in the first place?"

Noting that wardens' wives were sometimes offered words of "encouragement" such as "It must be nice to have a husband who is his own boss and works his own hours because he must spend lots of time with you and the kids," Anderson commented: "If ever a warden's wife goes off the deep end and beats some misguided soul half to death it will be after that profound statement has been uttered!"

Some officers are inclined to over-react to any perceived negative comment about wardens' spouses. Retired C.O. Tom Logan recalled an outburst from a U.S. warden at a "border warden" conference at Superior, Wisconsin, some years ago.

"I made an affectionate reference to my wife, Christine, as 'my old lady,'" said Logan. "Well, the warden suddenly got very excited and started attacking me verbally. 'Don't you dare call her that!' he shouted at me. 'That woman of yours is a queen. Any woman who sticks with a game warden for more than ten years deserves a medal....'"

Of course, ever since women have been employed as conservation officers, any warden's husband has had to learn to be just as long-suffering as a warden's wife. For Ed Boudreau, husband of Margaret Reed, Ontario's first woman C.O., the only problem lay in ensuring that his wife called him when she was out on assignment. "I used to worry about her sometimes," he said. "But now that she makes sure she calls me, it's O.K."

The home front can also be extended to include the local community, of which the warden is an integral part. In fact, the dependability and resourcefulness of the game warden has been so central to community life that many officers' names have been perpetuated in geographical landmarks. Billings Lake in Algonquin Park, for example, was inspired by officer Jack Billings who died nearby in mysterious circumstances while tracking a suspect in 1926. In May, 1989, an island in the St. Lawrence River was named after Royal Baker, a First World War veteran who became an overseer in 1921 and died in 1954 while employed as fish and wildlife supervisor at Kemptville.

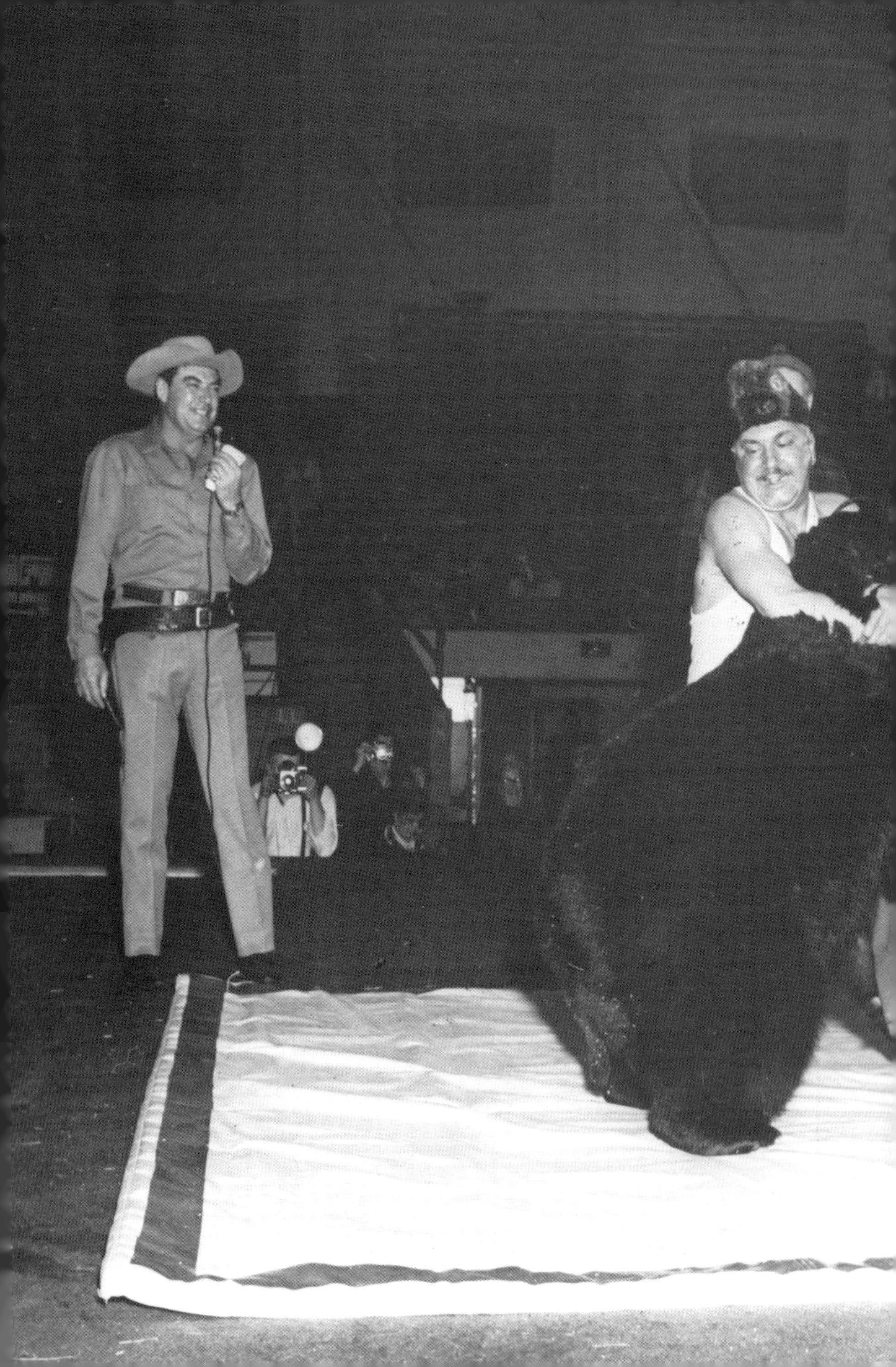

Chapter Thirteen: The Lighter Side

A sense of humour has always been of inestimable value to a conservation officer. Whether or not an officer has a well-developed sense of humour, life has a way of placing funny and bizarre incidents in the line of duty. So the officer who can accept—better still, enjoy—a touch of comedy is most likely to emerge smiling and unscathed from the most serious of situations. If laughter is the best medicine, warden Ernie Young of Blind River dispensed many spoonfuls in his day. A rugged Second World War veteran, Young became a living legend far beyond his patrol area by initiating one crazy exploit after another. Usually, his spirited high jinks were laced with a streak of zany exhibitionism.

Stocky and strong with twinkling eyes and a handlebar moustache, Young was a lovable rogue who liked nothing better than to surprise people and make them laugh even as he carried out his job.

Once, wearing full uniform, Young set out on water skis to patrol the massed ranks of astonished anglers. On another occasion, he disrobed—save for his underwear and C.O.'s peaked cap—and swam 200 yards into Lake Huron's North Channel to inspect the licences of anglers fishing from a boat.

INSET: *C.O. Ernie Young. His spirited high jinks were laced with a streak of zany exhibitionism.*
LEFT: *The lovable rogue in action. C.O. Ernie Young wrestles a bear at the Detroit Sportsmen's Show in March, 1968. The bear won but Ernie, as usual, made people laugh.*

While mounted on a horse and dressed as Santa Claus—a favourite annual ritual—Young rode into Blind River's Harmonic Hotel. Unfortunately, the establishment had tiled floors; the horse's steel shoes were covered in slush, and Young tumbled unceremoniously to the ground. The horse panicked and had to be blindfolded before it could be led back into the street. At a Detroit sports show, he wrestled bare-chested with a black bear. He dressed up in diapers as the New Year's baby at a local fishermen's ball.

"Ernie was a most colourful fellow," said Al MacFadyen, who worked as Young's partner in Blind River during the late 1960s. "He had a showboat personality—he loved to be the centre of attention. But he also really loved people and having fun and he worked as hard as he played."

All jest aside, Young was an exceptionally dedicated officer and, in the words of retired C.O. John McDonald, "nothing was too tough for Ernie." But his antics and contempt for bureaucracy landed him on the carpet before many disciplinary committees.

Young's boundless enthusiasm and conviviality concealed the tragedy in his life. While serving with the Hastings and Prince Edward Regiment during the war (when he converted the exhaust manifold of his armoured personnel carrier into a portable distillery!) he suffered a severe shrapnel wound that left him with a steel plate in his temple and a plague of headaches for years to come. The well-loved and much-respected officer retired in 1977 and died of stomach cancer in August, 1985.

Sometimes conservation officers *need* to have exemplary senses of humour. Harold Cantelon recalls confronting a "pregnant granny" in 1945 while helping a fellow warden search a household near Mount Forest suspected of taking wild mink out of season.

"It was dusk," Cantelon began, "and the man of the house was not home. The suspected poacher's wife let us in and introduced us to her grandmother, who looked pregnant and acted rather evasively. We wondered if the old woman might be hiding something under her apron.

"Bearing that in mind, we began to search the downstairs rooms. When we found nothing, I went upstairs to check the second floor. Grandma followed me from room to room until there was only one door left. 'Where does this lead to?' I asked. Receiving no reply, I impatiently opened the door, tripped on the threshold, and found myself outside, falling. I landed on all fours in an open sewage pit. Fortunately, I was only winded and a trifle startled.

"My partner's flashlight shone on me. 'What the hell are you doing down there?' he said. 'Don't worry about me,' I said. 'Look after Grandma.'

"His reply was reassuring. He said Grandma had laughed so hard when

I fell that six mink pelts had slipped out from under her apron. I managed to climb out from the smelly pit under my own steam, but was not allowed into our vehicle until I had cleaned myself up somewhat. I did and, wrapped in a blanket that we happened to have along, rode back to Mount Forest with my soiled uniform safely stowed in the trunk."

As for Grandma, she pleaded guilty.

C.O. Tim Boyd also plunged into a vat filled to the brim with noxious slime. When the incident happened, he was trekking across farmland with a high school student in search of possible baiting sites to trap wild turkeys for a management programme. It was a cool February morning in 1988. Taking a short cut behind a barn, Boyd suddenly found himself up to his armpits in a large pit of cow manure. The nasty surprise was concealed by a thin film of snow as well as snowbanks piled against the trough's sides. Luckily for Boyd, he was wearing his supervisor's floater coat.

> **Boyd suddenly found himself up to his armpits in a large pit of cow manure.**

"I couldn't even touch bottom," he lamented. "It was scary, really scary—I was treading the stuff to stay afloat. All I can say is that it's a good thing I wasn't running at the time!"

Holding a stick across the mire, the student hauled the rankly smelling officer back to dry land. Boyd then jumped into his ministry truck, drove the mile to his home, tore off his clothes and jumped gratefully into the shower. By the time he returned to Niagara District Office, his colleagues were ready for some fun. In the lunch room they mounted a "survival kit" display consisting of a snorkel, a pair of chest waders, a floater coat and some inflated balloons. When Boyd left Niagara to take a job as enforcement coordinator in Huronia District in May, 1988, the incident was revived for more laughs.

In April, 1968—just before the opening of the pickerel season—C.O.s Paddy Hogan and Jim Moore happened upon a carload of anglers in Consecon, Prince Edward County, whom they had wanted to apprehend for some time. Moore, who was driving, became so excited at this fortunate interception that he jammed the cruiser's controls into "reverse" instead of "park" and the patrol car slid down a large embankment into a ditch.

Just then, one of the anglers ran across the road and—holding down his head to remain anonymous—held up a large string of pickerel and yelled: "Are you looking for these, guys?" By the time the officers had clambered from the cruiser, the culprits were long gone.

The poachers, of course, don't always get the last laugh. In March, 1980, C.O. Brett Hodsdon charged a Lake Scugog resident for ice fishing with more than two lines. During the conversation that followed, the man mentioned that a couple of weeks earlier he had caught a yellow pickerel that contained a radio transmitter. Indeed, twenty-five cigar-sized transmitters had recently been surgically implanted in yellow pickerel in order to study their movements throughout the watershed.

The man, however, failed to show up for his court hearing and further attempts to locate him revealed he had given Hodsdon a correct name but a false address. Chatting about this dilemma in the Lindsay District Office coffee shop, fellow C.O. Bob Dyke mentioned that the transmitter was possibly still operational and said that, if the accused person lived in town, the beeping device could surely be located at his home. "I think it's worth a gamble," said Dyke.

So the two officers quickly installed the receiving equipment in a cruiser and the search began. Within ten minutes, a signal was detected and its strength placed the transmitter inside a house nearby. Hodsdon went to the front door and Dyke waited at the back just in case the resident should decide to flee.

As it happened, the man answered the knock at the front door and was so surprised to see Hodsdon that he made a full confession. It turned out that the man had long since eaten the fish containing the transmitter and had left the battery-operated item on a kitchen shelf. Incidentally, the transmitter, worth $250, was reused the following year in another study of pickerel migrations in the Kawartha Lakes.

Conservation officers love to enlist an element of surprise wherever possible and some will walk a long way with that aim in mind. The lake trout season had yet to begin in May, 1985, when Tom Logan pulled up in his ministry vehicle to spy figures on the far shore of Greenwater Lake, south of Shebandowan, about three kilometres away. Through his binoculars, he could see a camp, two men fishing, and a woman and some children nearby.

Logan reasoned that if he were to jump into his boat, the journey to the camp would take perhaps fifteen minutes. The anglers would spot him easily and have plenty of time to dispose of any evidence. Logan decided to walk around the lake behind the treeline—a much longer journey. Returning to his truck, he retrieved his "pinch" books, packed an orange and took a long drink from a water bottle. Then he set out.

The trek was long and arduous. Logan tramped for three hours picking his way around bushes and over tree stumps. At last he smelled woodsmoke and decided to walk a little farther so that he could approach the camp from the north side, where the wilderness lay, for maximum effect. He paused to remove twigs from his holster, combed his hair, put on his tie and straightened his uniform. Then, casually, he sauntered out to meet the group.

"Howdy!" said Logan. "How many lake trout do you have here?"

The older man's face blanched. Speechless, he stood and stared. The younger man recovered more quickly to reply: "We only got a few pike." (It was open season for pike.)

But Logan held the advantage of ambush and he could feel their uncertainty. Their bemused expressions told him there were lake trout nearby and a brief search turned up some lake trout fillets, neatly packed in a cooler. Charges followed against the two men for fishing out of season.

To maintain his aura of mystery, Logan left the group by walking up the beach and back into the northern wilderness before circling back to the truck. Once out of sight, he lay down in the undergrowth and laughed uncontrollably. The two men were duly convicted.

Neil MacNaughtan, who served as a warden during the 1920s, was proud of his reputation for turning up unexpectedly where his presence was least desired. Once, he hid close to a pickerel spawning bed so remotely situated that no poacher would ever suspect a game warden could possibly be nearby.

Night fell, and eventually a man appeared, shining a flashlight in the water. MacNaughtan waited until the man speared a pickerel immediately below his hiding place—then leaped down the river bank and grabbed the fellow before he could bolt in the darkness.

Startled out of his wits, the poacher exclaimed: "Jesus Christ!" To which MacNaughtan coolly replied: "No, just Neil NacNaughtan."

Alas, the humour of a situation is often lost on those caught breaking the law. While on a routine patrol in January, 1976, C.O.s Bob Partridge and Dave Marks were checking the ice fishing on Raleigh Lake, about sixteen kilometres west of Ignace. There, sixty metres offshore, were two set but unattended ice-fishing tip-ups. A cabin with a man sitting beside a large picture window overlooked the scene.

The officers went up to the cabin and explained to the owner, who was accompanied by a Siberian husky, that he must tend his lines at all times, patiently advising him that the lines must be withdrawn if he were to leave. The man assured the officers that his lines were being pulled out every evening.

Although doubting his word, the officers decided not to force the issue and left. Within a week, several complaints were received at the district office that this particular man was, indeed, leaving his lines set overnight.

With a humorous response in mind, Partridge and Marks decided to work the graveyard shift. At midnight, they were back on Raleigh Lake carrying a package of juicy bones to pacify the man's Siberian husky. Sure enough, they found the set lines lying unattended just as the husky bounded out on the ice to accept their peace offering. Then they hauled up one of the lines, attached a summons in a waterproof bag, loaded the line with gill net weights and lowered it back through the ice hole.

Next morning, the officers returned early to witness, from hiding, the angler's reaction. At 7:00 a.m., having spotted the sagging line, he strode excitedly across the ice to see what he had caught. After pulling up the bagged summons, "he huffed and he puffed, grabbed his minnow pail and marched back angrily to his cabin," said Partridge. The C.O.s, meanwhile, "were laughing too hard to show ourselves."

Later that day, the man stormed into Ignace District Office demanding to know whether the summons was a prank. District manager Terry Dodds explained that, although the summons was delivered in an unorthodox fashion, the charge itself was no joke. The man grimly paid his fine—without a trace of amusement!

In May, 1966, C.O.s Murray Martin and Bob Easton were patrolling Lake St. Francis, near Lancaster, when they confronted three anglers. Two of them were bearing expired four-day licences and the third had no licence at all. The officers told the third man—who was about thirty years old and balding—that they would be seizing his fishing equipment. The man reacted by putting up his fists and declaring that they must fight him first.

Not wanting to provoke an unnecessary brawl, the officers retired to shore and called the O.P.P. The man was subsequently picked up and placed in Cornwall jail for three nights over the long weekend. On Tuesday morning, charged with fishing without a licence and obstructing peace officers, the bald-headed angler appeared before a judge in Alexandria. The man told the court that he wasn't really fishing with a hook and line but had only a bent nail.

"Why?" demanded the judge, who also happened to be bald.

"My head is similar to yours, Your Honour," the man replied. "Everyone knows that grass can grow just about anywhere. I was just trying to hook some weeds from the bottom of the lake so that I could squeeze the juice from them and rub it on my head." The fifty people in the courtroom roared with laughter. Everyone laughed, in fact, except the judge.

Officer Easton was recalled to the stand and questioned as to what was on the end of the man's line. When he answered "a red and white daredevil," the fast-talking defendant's fate was sealed. The judge told him: "You must have lain awake in jail all weekend to dream up a story like that."

In yet another fishing story, C.O. Freeman "Smoky" Cole was on the lookout for pickerel poachers on the banks of the Hut River, which flows beside the hamlet of Silver Dollar. It was the spring of 1977 and Cole and his black Labrador, Tara, were hidden by a blind of brush and balsam boughs. From this vantage point, Cole noticed a local citizen bend over suspiciously to wash something in the river and clean off a fillet knife. The man stood up and looked around to ensure that he was not being observed before reaching into the grass for a plastic bag. He then placed a number of filleted fish in the bag, undid the belt of his pants, placed the bag inside his trousers and tied it to his belt buckle before covering up the deception with a wool jacket.

At this point, Cole and Tara left the blind and went to hide behind the man's parked vehicle. The C.O. stood up just as the poacher was about to drive away.

"I couldn't resist having a little fun," said Cole. "I told the guy that he was putting on a lot of weight. He agreed, saying that the length of the winter had helped to add a few pounds. But I could tell he was getting more and more nervous and beads of sweat were standing out on his brow. Eventually, I went straight to the point and he admitted everything. He undid his pants and produced eight fillets—four yellow pickerel—from the bag."

At least the offender—a local restaurant owner—had the good grace to appreciate the lighter side. Years later, Cole visited the man's restaurant and there, hanging in his office, was a framed cartoon showing a guilt-stricken man with fishtails jutting from his pants in company with Smoky Cole the warden and Tara, the black Labrador.

Lawbreakers who are easily fooled by a C.O.'s broad grin are asking for trouble. In response to complaints regarding a local aircraft and its use for moose hunting, C.O. Joan Hubay and M.N.R. biologist Lori Butterfield were despatched to Ragged Wood Lake, north of Sioux Lookout, in September, 1986. There, the two women, posing as hunters, met up with four hunters from Toronto and were right on the spot when one of the men killed a moose illegally. The successful hunter proudly took a photograph (with Hubay's camera) of Hubay and Butterfield posing with the dead animal.

"He thought we were smiling because he had shot the moose," said Hubay. "But we weren't at all. We were smiling because we were thinking: 'We've got you now!'" And so they had. The four men were subse-

FIGURE 13-1
"We've got you now!" C.O. Joan Hubay (right) and M.N.R. biologist Lori Butterfield pose with an illegally slaughtered moose north of Sioux Lookout in September, 1986. The picture helped to convict the hunters who were responsible for the kill.

quently fined a total of $2,215 for unlawfully hunting moose.

"We've got you now!" were exactly the words uttered by C.O. Jim Ives while on poacher patrol close to midnight in April, 1971. In company with an O.P.P. officer, Ives had descended on a pair of lawbreakers in Melville Creek, Prince Edward County.

"We arrested one guy and seized his car containing fish on the bridge at Melville," said Ives. "But another guy ran through the river and got away."

Ives then asked the O.P.P. officer to drive the seized vehicle—a "beat-up wreck" with a loud muffler—while the arrested man sat beside him with Ives hidden in the back seat. The trio had driven for about five kilometres when they heard someone hollering from way off in a field. When the car stopped, the man who had fled ran up to the vehicle barefoot, having lost his shoes in the river.

"How many did they get?" he inquired breathlessly on reaching the car window.

Chuckled Ives: "We've got *you* now."

A keen sense of smell has led many a warden to concealed evidence over the years. Reg "Bullet Head" Windsor, who was fish and wildlife supervisor at Thunder Bay during the 1940s, would regularly offer trappers and their wives transportation in his black Ford automobile. If the trappers had more pelts than they were allowed or if fur-bearing animals had been killed in closed season, their wives would sometimes wear these illegal pelts around their midriffs in wintertime. Knowing this, Windsor would turn up the car's heater, which quickly activated the odour of fur and allowed him to sniff out any wrongdoing.

In the cause of duty, Ed Skuce made some exaggerated claims for his nose one fall near Powassan in the 1940s. Skuce was out on patrol when, unseen, he witnessed some deer hunters shooting out-of-season grouse. He waited until the men had returned to camp and then casually strolled into their midst on what was, ostensibly, a routine visit. After chatting for a while, Skuce raised his head and sniffed the air.

"I can smell grouse," he told the assembled company.

Astonished denials followed, there was further conversation, and—again—Skuce sniffed the air.

"I'm *positive* I can smell grouse," he declared.

This time, the warden set off on a meandering search of the camp that led, eventually, to a cache of dead grouse and some shamefaced hunters. The incident won Skuce a reputation as the sharpest nose for miles around.

The next story serves as a warning to every loudmouth who has ever boasted of his prowess in the great outdoors.

It was about 10:00 p.m. in late February, 1974, and patrolling C.O. Will Samis and his large Irish wolfhound, Byron, were returning to base by snow machine. They were about forty-eight kilometres north of Elliot

Lake when Samis noticed a glimmer of light from a normally empty cabin.

Just to make sure that everything was all right, he parked his machine on the main trail, opting to walk the few hundred metres to the cabin. It was snowing heavily as Byron padded on ahead and by the time Samis neared the cabin he could hear, faintly at first, a strange high-pitched chanting. The sound was so unusual that Samis decided to identify the noise before announcing himself. As he got closer, the sound—ranging from a half-hearted whistle to an almost tearful dirge—was interspersed with Byron's loud, grunted sniffs. When the cabin came into view, Samis could see the back of a large man standing with his feet apart as if he were trying to relieve himself. Byron was standing behind him with his nose in the man's crotch, a favourite pastime of this odour-loving hound.

When Samis called Byron to his side, the man—visibly shaken—almost collapsed with relief. Then, followed by the officer, he staggered in through the cabin door where the light showed that his face had drained of all colour. Inside were the man's wife and another couple and, for some time, Samis could neither understand the man's state of alarm nor why his companions were convulsing with laughter. His wife, in particular, was overjoyed. "Serves you right!" she said, over and over again.

When the commotion eventually died down and the man, Malcolm (a pseudonym) had been treated for shock, Samis was given an explanation for his unconventional behaviour. He learned that Malcolm's wife, Linda (a pseudonym), was making her first winter visit from Michigan to the northern cabin. Malcolm, apparently, had bragged endlessly of his abilities as a woodsman and had convinced her that local wolves were dangerous—especially without his constant protection.

An hour before Byron and Samis came along, Linda had plucked up sufficient courage to venture to the outdoor toilet. Though frightened by Malcolm's stories, she was persuaded that, this time, she would be safe. But in the middle of her ritual, the sound of howling wolves had sent her running in terror for the safety of the cabin. Malcolm, who had done the howling himself, had laughed long and cruelly.

Malcolm knew, of course, that wolves often respond to a human call and when he, in turn, stepped out to relieve himself and suddenly felt Byron's nose in his crotch, he was convinced a wolf had answered his invitation. After all, he had no idea that any other humans, or dogs for that matter, were within a dozen kilometres of the cabin. As he admitted later, the door of the cabin was only six metres away but fear had paralysed him.

As for that strange chanting, Malcolm had read somewhere that the sound of a gentle human voice would calm a wild animal and nervous chanting was the best he could muster under the circumstances!

> **Just to make sure that everything was all right, he parked his machine on the main trail, opting to walk the few hundred metres to the cabin.**

FISH AND WILD LIFE
INFORMATION

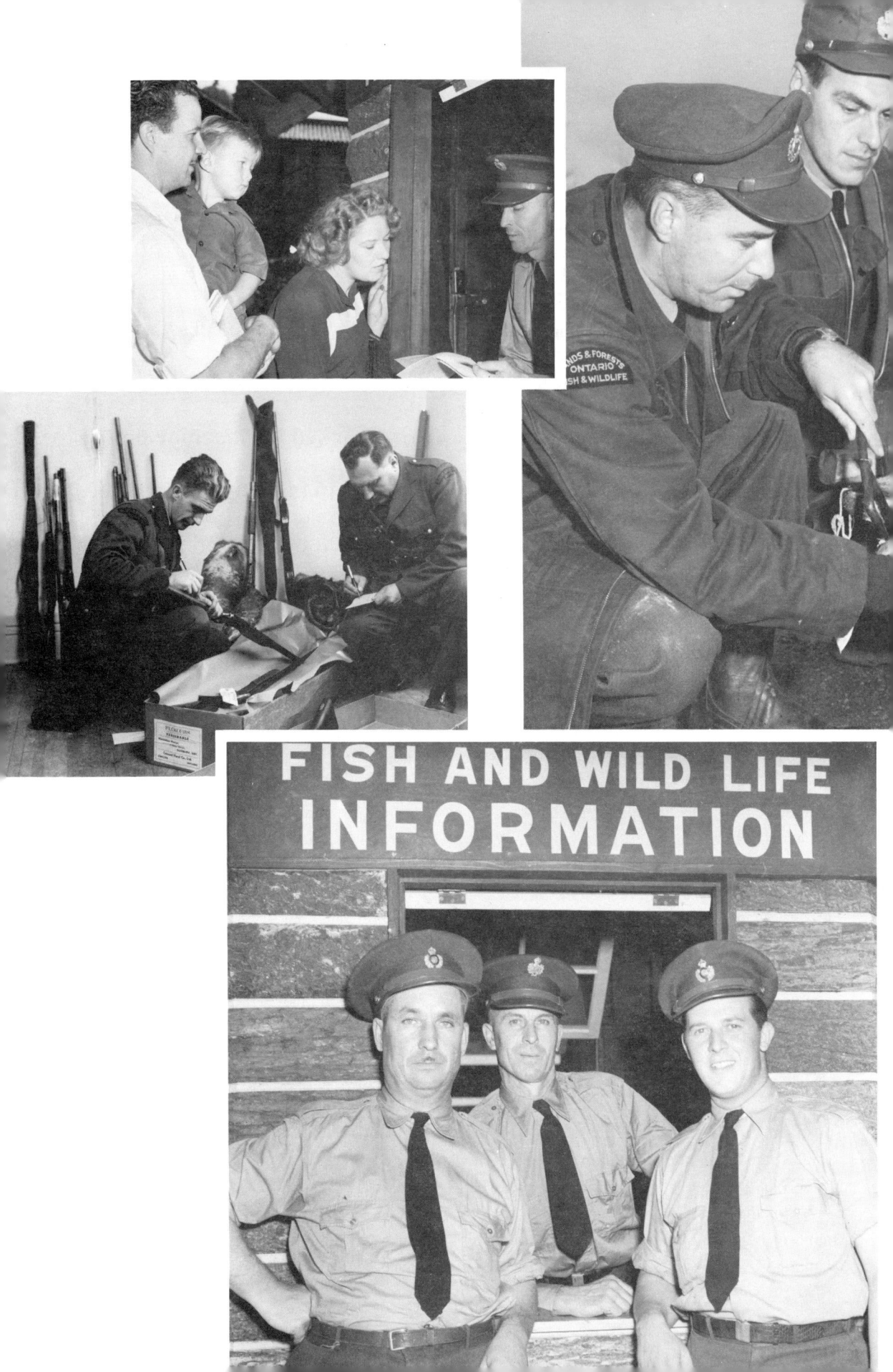

Chapter Fourteen: Looking Back

By John Macfie and Carl Monk, veteran C.O's

LEFT: *Fond memories contributed by staff and friends.*

No Bed of Roses
by John Macfie

To dispel any lingering notion that the lot of the conscientious conservation officer was a bed of roses, I want to describe incidents from the lives of two officers of my close acquaintance, Neil MacNaughtan and Ernie Bain.

Working out of Parry Sound, Neil MacNaughtan administered fish and game law throughout Parry Sound and Muskoka districts—at the outset single-handedly—for forty years prior to retiring in 1960. Fur-bearing animals were paramount among the concerns of the game and fishery overseer of the 1920s and 1930s. It reflected the times: wild fur represented the epitome of luxury in the fashion world. Populations of most species were for one reason or another at low levels, and a single raw skin of a beaver could be worth as much as a man might earn by toiling for a whole month in one of the region's lumber camps. A top-grade fisher pelt, the pot of gold at the end of every trapper's rainbow, was so valuable that on those rare occasions when a track was discovered, the animal was trailed until it was treed or cornered in a den. It was this state of affairs that enabled an English romantic named Archie Belaney to imprint his name indelibly in Canadian folklore by adopting some young beavers and writing stories about them under the pen name "Grey Owl."

FIGURE 14-1
John Macfie, 1987.

To the game warden of 1925, who could not in his wildest dreams have foreseen a day to come when the beaver would be just another rodent, a suspected case of beaver poaching was a matter of the greatest urgency. The following expanded version of Neil's diary pages for February, 1925, and subsequent events, reconstructed from a memoir I taped a few years before his death in 1988, will provide a sense of the effort involved in tracking down a poacher in the packsack and snowshoe days.

Neil had been tipped off that three men suspected of having illegal beaver pelts in their possession had been seen boarding a C.N.R. train at the wilderness flag stop of Still River, sixty kilometres north of Parry Sound. So severe an allegation prompted him to call on the assistance of his counterpart at Lindsay, Reg Windsor, and early on the morning of February 5, the two hoisted packs and struck off in an easterly direction from the C.N.R. tracks at Bolger Bridge, twenty kilometres short of Still River. Their carefully planned strategy was to capture their quarry in a roundhouse assault from the rear.

Nightfall found them taking welcome shelter under the roof of Jack Campbell's lumber camp on Partridge Lake in Wilson Township, about thirty-five kilometres from Bolger Bridge and about as remote a spot as you could find in Parry Sound District, then or today. Next day, MacNaughtan and Windsor pressed on with their plan to blindside their suspects by looping back westward for twenty-one kilometres to Windy Lake, as the diary records, there to supper and sleep in another lumber camp.

On Saturday, the officers' wide right hook connected. Information gleaned at the lumber camp zeroed them in on a shack whose furnishings amounted to little more than a pair of old mattresses between which all three of their quarry were bedded down when the officers walked in.

When a search of the premises yielded no incriminating furs, MacNaughtan and Windsor hit the trail again, this time for a deer-hunting camp on Noganosh Lake, further up the Still River. The camp, it was revealed in their questioning of the group, was also used for shelter in their wilderness wanderings. That day's journey, it will be noted, amounted to twenty-six kilometres.

Readers who have never had the pleasure of snowshoeing and carrying a pack thirty-five kilometres—or even only twenty-one kilometres—in one day have the writer's assurance that it can leave one weary and footsore. But remember this was long ago when an offence involving a beaver was a national outrage.

No furs were to be found in the deer hunters' camp either, and after bunking there for the night, the officers decided to call it quits—for then. They were now back to within ten kilometres as the crow flies of the C.N.R. stop at Drocourt. However, water lying on the sprawling arms of Noganosh Lake forced the men to take the long way around, so it would not be until late the following afternoon, after five days and five nights out, that they climbed aboard a train for Parry Sound—empty-handed.

But if the poachers believed they were off the hook, they underestimated the doggedness and dedication to the job of game and fishery overseer Neil MacNaughtan. When he left the hunting camp on Noganosh Lake, Neil carried in his pocket the business card of a Sudbury fur-buyer, which he had spied tucked in a window sash. Late that month he journeyed to Sudbury and examined the records of this and other dealers, and upon returning to Parry Sound laid information before Police Magistrate Broughton against all three individuals.

With O.P.P. Constable Purvis along for assistance, Neil took the train north and at the shack where he had first found the three, arrested two of them. The third, he learned, could probably be found at the hunting camp on Noganosh Lake. After conducting the two out to the track at Drocourt, where he left them in the custody of Purvis, Neil again struck off into the bush for the hunting camp ten kilometres distant—and returned with the third poacher in tow, just in time to watch the southbound way freight pull out with Purvis and his charges aboard.

With O.P.P. Constable Purvis along for assistance, Neil took the train north and at the shack where he had first found the three, arrested two of them.

FIGURE 14-2
Warden Neil MacNaughtan: dogged and dedicated.

"Therefore," Neil told me, "we had to wait for the afternoon train, go up to Ludgate, walk across to Pakesley and come down on the train arriving at two o'clock in the morning. I brought [the prisoner] home, but I didn't give him a bed because I wasn't too sure whether he had cooties or not."

He and his prisoner had caught the northbound way freight at Drocourt, got off where the C.N.R. and C.P.R. tracks crossed and walked three kilometres up the track to the C.P.R. station at Pakesley, where they boarded the only passenger train that could land them in Parry Sound in time for court the following day.

Summary justice prevailed at the time. Neil often marched violators directly to court from where he apprehended them, and most of his cases were disposed of within twenty-four hours. So it was with the Still River poachers. One of the trio, who made a clean breast of things and in doing so implicated his partners, was fined $60, the others $90 and $120. The last mentioned, revealed by Neil's sifting of fur-buyers' records to have sold an otter as well as beavers, chose the option of two months in jail. The choice was probably not altogether voluntary, for $120 was more money than most people could lay their hands on in 1925.

A conservative estimate of the distance Neil MacNaughtan walked, a large part of it through wilderness on snowshoes, in apprehending and bringing to justice those three beaver poachers, is 125 kilometres.

But in those days, that was no big deal.

In my own generation, the era in which the game warden assumed the dual role of both enforcement officer and resource manager, Ernie Bain pulled off this balancing act with extreme dexterity. Soon after joining the Department of Lands and Forests in 1957, Ernie began gaining attention as an innovator and practitioner of deer range manipulation techniques, and by the time he retired thirty-one years later, he was recognized as the

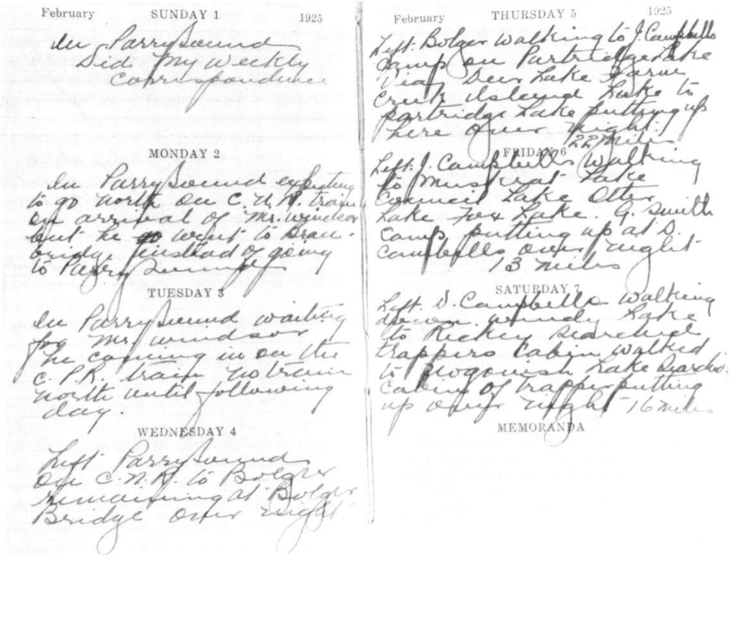

FIGURE 14-3
Neil MacNaughtan's diary of February 1 to 7, 1925, records how he tracked down beaver poachers in the packsack and snowshoe days.

province's foremost authority on nursing snow-beleaguered deer through hard winters. Yet when required he slipped easily into his enforcement alter ego—all too often after supper following a full day's work on the biological side of conserving fish and wildlife.

The fact that Ernie worked out of the tiny rural community, Loring, in which he was born and raised, knowing and known to everyone in his patrol area, provided incentive to excel: he could hardly afford to do less than his very best. But his natural makeup included an extra measure of determination to succeed in the face of adversity, come hell or cold water, as the following incident will show.

Caribou Lake, set in the wilderness west of Loring, measures one and one-half by seven kilometres, and harbours in its fifty-metre depths a population of lake trout whose spawning season happens to coincide with the annual deer hunt. One November night in the early 1960s, Ernie apprehended two poachers who had speared a pair of those trout in their moment of reproductive bliss. He discovered the culprits were from a deer camp at the remote end of the lake, so he made haste there, searched the building and found another large spawner secreted under the camp's bread supply. The poachers paid their fines. Then a couple of years later Ernie narrowly missed nailing the same gang at the same game.

The fact that his earlier lesson in game fish conservation had gone unheeded bared the bulldog streak in Ernie Bain.

One hour before midnight on November 3, 1965, the tip he was waiting for arrived in a telephone call from a tourist outfitter on Caribou Lake. Winking lights were visible on the spawning bed. Ernie summoned Deputy Conservation Officer Bob Lampman to meet him at the Loring Deputy Chief Ranger Headquarters, where they quickly loaded a canoe on a pickup truck. In their haste, Ernie remembered to return to the warehouse for lifejackets, only as they were about to pull away. It proved to be a life-saving afterthought.

By the time they reached and quietly paddled across Caribou Lake to the spawning bed, no one was around. Had the hunters again managed to spear their deer season feast of illicit trout? Examination of their boat would likely give the answer, one way or another. So the two men paddled to the west end of the lake where, by creeping along the shore and examining the boat's interior with a flashlight shielded inside his parka, Ernie determined that all the paraphernalia—a fish spear, an underwater light and battery—were there, but no tell-tale spawn or blood from a speared fish. Perhaps the trout were not yet on the spawning bed. A check by flashlight, now that there was no fear of tipping their hand, would reveal if there were fish in shallow water.

> **Ernie remembered to return to the warehouse for lifejackets, only as they were about to pull away. It proved to be a life-saving afterthought.**

Back at the spawning bed Ernie and Bob located only two skittish trout, the advance party of the spawning run to come. The poachers from the deer camp would be sure to be back on succeeding nights. It was now past two o'clock in the morning. After scouting a spot to hide their canoe and lie in wait next time, the officers struck off directly across Caribou Lake to begin a journey home that Ernie now picks up:

"It was my fault. We should have got down on our knees, but it was cold. Six inches* of snow had fallen, and the wind had been north all day. We could feel ice on the paddles. Bob said to me, 'I'm that cold I have no feeling left in my legs.'

"I don't know to this day what happened, whether Bob went to shift on the thwart, but his hand just came up like that. If I had been on my knees I think I could have caught the canoe, but the next thing we were in the lake. I said to Bob, 'Get your lifejacket and put it on.' And I said, 'All water safety says to stay with the canoe, but at three o'clock in the morning nobody is going to see us, and they aren't going to be looking for us before ten o'clock in the morning. By that time we are just going to be floating corpses.'

"We were at about the centre of the lake. I said, 'Come on Bob, let's go.' He said, 'No.' I tried to reason with him, but he said, 'No, I'm staying with the canoe.' So I struck out. Every once in a while I'd give a yell, 'Come on Bob!' But finally I thought I'm just losing steam by this, and I just swam. The stars were bright and I kept the north star at my back. I had a back operation that spring and I was worried when I got to shore I'd be so stiff I couldn't walk. Of course I didn't know if I was even going to get to shore. But finally my hand hit something and I crawled out, and I was on shore. I would say I was twenty-five minutes, maybe half an hour in the lake.

"I made a mistake, I took my coat off and the cold really hit me. I had a mile to go, more by the time you go along the shore and over the cliffs. My back was really bothering me. But I had a hill to go over and that seemed to loosen it up. I remember getting to the truck and getting in and turning it around, and I remember turning the corner when I came out of the Caribou Lake road, then the next thing I was stopped in Loring, shaking my head and wondering what—where am I? Then I remembered Bob's out in the lake. I went home, and I don't remember whether I peeped the horn or what, but Marion [Mrs. Bain] came and helped me out of the truck."

A rescue party headed by Provincial Police Constable Doug Cornwall raced to Caribou Lake, and patrolled the shore by boat in a thick fog that had now settled in. They discovered the lifejacket Ernie had left at the water's edge as a marker, and a little beyond that was a human form lying on

FIGURE 14-4
C.O. Ernie Bain examines a freshly shed deer antler in Loring deeryard, 1970.

---
* 2.5 centimetres = 1 inch

a sloping rock, barely above the water line. It was Bob Lampman who, spurred by Ernie's determined example, had changed his mind and followed in his wake. Bob emerged from the hospital a few days later suffering no more injury than torn toe-nails and finger-nails from clawing his way up the icy rock.

As for Ernie, his final memory of that terrible night is of asking Marion to find him an outfit of dry clothes in which to return to Caribou Lake to rescue Bob. Then a needle administered by the doctor Marion had summoned took effect, and by the time he awoke, his nightmare had come to a happy conclusion.

Fun and Games
by Carl Monk

FIGURE 14-5
Carl Monk, 1991.

It was a pleasant, summery day in June, 1951. Lake Superior in the vicinity of Caribou Island was unusually calm. Beneath what little wave there was, the seven varieties of lake trout held sway over the population of herring, chub, whitefish, sucker and sculpin.

About twenty-seven kilometres to the east of Caribou Island, the captain of the patrol boat *Haywood* scanned the waters with binoculars. Captain Ed Nicholson was a dedicated sailor and knew Lake Superior well, having spent several years steering large freighters to and from the Lakehead. "There's a boat out there up to something," he said to engineer Bud Bennett of Sault Ste. Marie. "She's just on the horizon and I keep losing her. What do you say we check it out?"

"Suits me," replied Bennett.

Caribou Island is three kilometres as a seagull flies inside Canadian waters from the international boundary with the United States.

About two hours later, the *Haywood* pulled into the only harbour of Caribou Island. Lying at anchor was a commercial fishing tug from Michigan. Its crew looked somewhat menacing, to say the least. Nicholson was undismayed. "Heave to!" he shouted. "We're coming aboard."

"We're just here for a rest and to get out of the weather," the one who seemed to be in charge said. "Got our nets set about five miles* west of here on the Michigan side."

That's mistake number one, Nicholson thought. The weather is pretty calm.

"What're you fishing for?" asked Nicholson.

"Trout."

That's mistake number two, thought Nicholson. Trout season's closed in Michigan. At the same time, he glanced at the tug's charts lying on the map table next to the wheel.

* 1.6 kilometres = 1 mile

The *Haywood* backed off, turned around the point and headed southeast away from the island. After about seventeen minutes, Bennett turned the boat sharply ninety degrees. After another five minutes he cut the engine. "That net's got to be around here," said Nicholson, "unless I misread his charts." Bennett probed the water with a pike pole. Seconds later he snagged a line. The clank and screech of the ship's net-lifter echoed across the water as the crew began hauling a bait-hook line on board. Altogether about one and a half kilometres of line and half a tonne of lake trout were hoisted on board the deck of the *Haywood*. It was now evening and the sun was going down in the west.

> **The clank and screech of the ship's net-lifter echoed across the water as the crew began hauling a bait-hook line on board.**

Nicholson returned to the harbour at Caribou Island and tied up alongside the tug from Michigan. Moments later he advised the three commercial fishers they were under arrest for fishing in Ontario waters without a licence and for using set lines to take lake trout. The men were a surly lot; they refused to admit anything.

Next morning, Nicholson radioed the Department of Lands and Forests in Sault Ste. Marie. About two hours later a Beaver aircraft from Provincial Air Service with officers M.T. Watson and J.J. Bussineau on board landed in the harbour at Caribou Island. Shortly afterwards, the gang admitted the nets and hooks were theirs. "I have a large monthly payment to make on the tug's two new diesel engines and this was the quickest way I knew of making it," the one in charge stated. They were flown to the Sault and jailed to await court Monday morning at 10:00 a.m.

The fine was a paltry $100 apiece plus costs of $6. The commercial fishermen had been charged with angling without a licence, *not* with illegal commercial fishing (the number of hooks and length of line readily indicating a commercial operation). Notwithstanding the mistake, the Royal Canadian Mounted Police took charge of the seized (now forfeited following conviction) tug because it was deemed to be hovering in Canadian waters without benefit of having gone through customs. Thirty days later it was sold at public auction.

The following was told to me by Ed Nicholson and Bud Bennett in late September, 1951, when on board the *Haywood*, bound for Eagle River from the Michipicoten River.

On the Eagle River assignment, plans called for me to stake out the river and try to prevent commercial fishermen from Michigan seining there. When the spawning run was at its peak, it was possible to capture as much as a tonne of lake trout. The trout that ascended the mouth of the river were huge, up to sixteen kilograms or more. I had a hard time catching a small one to eat. I needed to eat because the *Haywood* had not returned to bring me any grub for a week. Since they put me off on a rock at the mouth of the Eagle River in the dark with only enough food for a couple of days, I was concerned something might have happened to them. It had—Nicholson had broken his wrist and had to go back to the Sault to have it set and a cast put on. Seems he had attempted to board the *Haywood* late at night with two cases of refreshments and had fallen. So much for the romance of sailing Lake Superior.

Later that fall of 1951, I was at Leamington in the banana belt of the province to assist in the pheasant hunt on Pelee Island and around Essex County. I worked with game and fishery overseers Del Bailey, Leamington; Gordon Greenwood, Essex; Tom Carter, Merlin; and supervisor Ed Skuce, Aylmer. They were good overseers to work with. There were plenty of pheasants then because there was lots of cover—dense, wide and well thorned and brambled fence rows, heavily grassed and vined woodlots and thickets, grain fields of all kinds with lots of weeds and grass between the rows. On the mainland in Essex County our main cases were for shooting hen birds and hunting without a township licence.

In November of that year, I was with overseer E.W. Ferguson, tracking down pre-season deer poachers in the wilds back of Griffith, several kilometres north of Kaladar. Bob Sheppard, the fish and wildlife supervisor in Tweed, had told me the gang of poachers we were after would use hounds and hunt on Sunday. He was right on both counts. When we caught up with them it was Sunday morning, the hounds (two blueticks and a walker) were tonguein', and the hunters were on watch at the runways. There were lots of deer in those days. The six and a half kilometres walk back to the main road with a pack of six rifles through a thirty centimetres of loose snow, however, was not all that much fun. While in eastern Ontario, I worked with some great overseers: John Shannon, Bob Davidson, Percy Thompson, Bruce Page and Jack Thibodeau. I also worked a couple of times with Forest Richardson. Forest was famous for breeding and raising Plott hounds and hunting wolves.

Six months later in May, 1952, I was again on a Greyhound bus heading for North Bay: yellow pickerel runs at Sturgeon Falls; beaver poaching in the Jocko Crown Game Preserve; huge speckled trout fishing at Emerald, Shanty and Jimmy Lakes between McLaren's Bay on Lake Temiskaming and Diver on the Ontario Northland Railway. During the winter of 1952/53, I was a spotter in a Beaver aircraft conducting a moose survey north of River Valley. Pilot George Philips from Algonquin Park was at the controls, and overseer Ted (Bear) Cusson was our navigator. Our tally was 167 moose. Henry Haskins was the fish and wildlife supervisor at North Bay. Other overseers included: Bill St. Pierre, Bill Cote, Aurelle Laundriault, Auguste Whissell and Ed Mantle at Haileybury. During those years, we usually caught about forty poachers taking yellow pickerel during the spring run from Lake Nipissing hot spots.

Most of 1954 was spent at Ranger School (now the Leslie M. Frost Natural Resources Centre) on the shores of St. Nora's Lake. The curriculum, sponsored and paid for by the Department of Lands and Forests, included such practical subjects as: surveying, fire fighting, tree/shrub identification by the twig, bark, log, bud, leaf, fruit and flower; timber cruising (estimating the amount of merchantable timber and how to get at it); telephone (hooking a copper line from tree to tree and post to post); snake, turtle, frog, fish, bird and mammal identification and management; resource laws and about thirty more interesting subjects. One of the best features of the school included the policies and practices of the department with respect to issue or refusal of various licences: trapping, tourist camps, guides, commercial fishing, bait fish vendors and others. Wolf and bear bounties were discussed and explained (overseers were responsible for the bounties paid for bear and wolves). Generally, the calibre of the instructors at the school and course content were outstanding. Furthermore, graduation from the thirty-three-week course entitled an overseer to advance from Group I to II, a salary increase of about $360 annually—a sizeable amount of money at the time. Ranger School was a plus for not only the overseer but also the public.

During the 1960s, I was surveying lakes and rivers, conducting moose, caribou and beaver surveys and running a goose camp in the Patricias

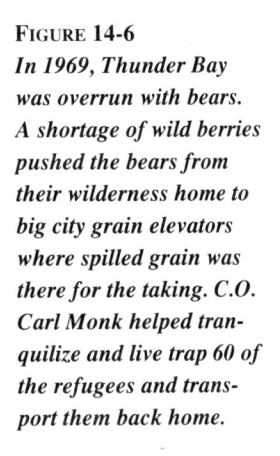

FIGURE 14-6
In 1969, Thunder Bay was overrun with bears. A shortage of wild berries pushed the bears from their wilderness home to big city grain elevators where spilled grain was there for the taking. C.O. Carl Monk helped tranquilize and live trap 60 of the refugees and transport them back home.

north of Sioux Lookout (about 725 kilometres north of the Sioux) at Fort Severn. Sioux Lookout was a vast hinterland full of game and fish: moose, caribou, polar bear, ptarmigan, sharp tail grouse, lake trout, sturgeon and goldeye.

Wages for conservation officers, however, had begun to slip in the 1960s. To offset declining funds, my family (my wife, four children and I) had to cut stove wood to keep warm during the winter, rather than pay for furnace oil, and make sure the freezer had one moose, one deer, several grouse, ducks, geese and fish packed and frozen for the winter months. During the summer and fall, we had to pick and can wild strawberries, blueberries, raspberries, saskatoons and whatever vegetables or fruit we could get from the garden. A sewing machine was used to make most of the children's clothing. Fresh eggs by the case, as well as some poultry, were shipped in on the freight train from Neepawa, Manitoba; freight rates at Sioux Lookout were subsidized by the federal government. You had to be innovative to be a game overseer in the 1960s.

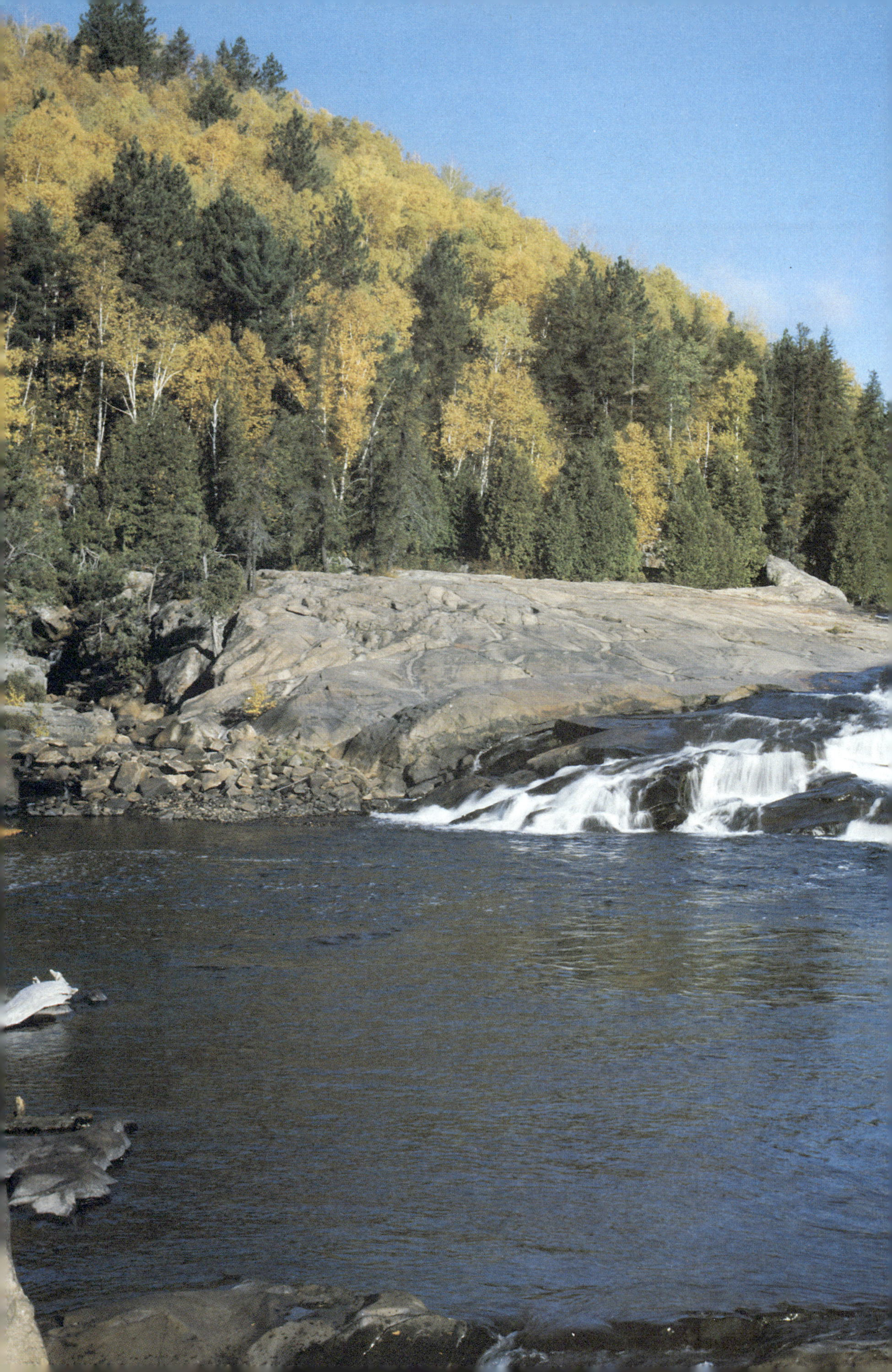

Chapter Fifteen: Last Words

When a Royal Commission recommended the creation of Algonquin Park in 1893, the second part of its report was prefaced by a haunting poem. The anonymous author is thought to be Alexander Kirkwood, commission chairman and the man who first proposed the founding of the park. Verse after verse laments the hideous destruction of the previous century and predicts the future ecological ruin of Ontario. The dread requiem for our natural resources concludes:

Great cities that had thriven marv'lously
Before their source of thrift was swept away
Faded and perished, as a plant will die
With water banished from its roots and leaves;
And men sate starving in their treeless waste
Beside their treeless farms and empty marts,
And wondered at the ways of Providence.

It's a grim vision and one that game wardens over the past century have been determined to avert at all costs. That they have made a magnificent contribution to this cause is reason enough to celebrate in 1992. But the battle wears on.

In this year of commemoration, conservation officers continue to confront the forces and influences that despoil our priceless heritage. As they do so, changes are taking place in the political philosophy

INSET: *C.O. Ken Henry. One member of the province-wide team that continues to confront the forces and influences despoiling our priceless heritage.*

that directs their actions. The key phrase pointing to the future of Ontario's natural resources is "sustainable development," a phrase that embraces continued economic development but only in so far as that development is both socially responsible and environmentally sensitive. "Our objective is to develop sustainability by protecting the integrity of our land and water base and the resources they support," said Andy Houser, director of the Compliance Policy Branch. "The old adage 'an ounce of prevention is worth a pound of cure' really does apply to issues of conservation."

Conservation officers can expect their expertise in enforcement, public relations and education to be more broadly based in the years ahead. As society evolves, currently Regional Director in Huntsville, Al Stewart sees C.O.s working in more of a partnership role with resource users. Self-policing, he feels, will become more prevalent in a variety of areas. "I think that because of peer pressure, fewer and fewer people will be found committing offences," he said. "We will still have to catch the hog but a new ethic will be in place."

The concept that the C.O.s' role would be enlarged was welcomed by Alan Farrer, president of the Ontario Conservation Officer's Association. Increased public education is necessary, he said, because—despite the growth in environmental awareness—many people are still ignorant about specific issues such as hunting and trapping, as well as the renewable aspect of Ontario's resources.

At the same time, Farrer could see officers being overtaxed with new responsibilities unless there was a commensurate increase in officer numbers. Farrer said it was vital that the current emphasis on enforcement at least be maintained as officers enter an intense period of change. "The public wants a strong enforcement presence," he declared.

The C.O.'s job seems destined to grow more complex as society itself becomes more culturally and technologically sophisticated. As officers across the province brace themselves for the next century of endeavour, there is every expectation that their tasks will be no less tough or challenging than before.

Only, perhaps, when a warden's career is over, retirement is done and the pearly gates beckon can there be a taste of well-earned rapture. To quote an anonymous poem, **Warden's Reward**:

A man knocked at the heavenly gate
His face was scarred and old;
He stood before the man of fate
For admission to the fold.
What have you done, St. Peter asked,
To gain admission here?
I have been a Game Warden, Sir,
For many and many a year.
The pearly gates swung open wide,
St. Peter touched the bell—
Come and choose your harp, he said,
You have had your share of hell.

Author's Aknowledgements

I would like to propose a personal toast to Ontario's conservation officers on the occasion of their centenary: "You Gameys have triumphed against all odds over the past 100 years. Congratulations! And may the next century smile on you."

In the course of researching and writing this book, I have been unfailingly impressed with the genuineness, courage, dedication, courtesy and good humour of each and every interviewed officer, past and present. Many are those who have contributed, but a special thanks is due for the assistance of the following: Dale Gartley, Gord Black, Carl Monk, Ian Anderson, Rick Stankiewicz, Brett Hodsdon, Charlie Bibby, Al MacFadyen and Bruce Tomlinson.

My appreciation extends also to researchers Kathy Dodge and Tom La Duron, Compliance Policy Branch secretary Karen Pukara, biologists Allan Wainio and Mike Buss, and to Doug Dodge, Great Lakes Fisheries Co-ordinator, for lending me his quiet, light-filled office overlooking Queen's Park. Finally, a verbal bouquet for my wife, Emily, who exhibited admirable patience and serenity throughout the project's eighteen weeks.

Photograph Acknowledgements

The Ministry of Natural Resources wishes to thank the following people for the contribution of their photographs.

Mr. Ian Anderson	Ministry of Natural Resources Archives
Mr. Ben Attard	Mr. Carl Monk
Mr. Steve Aubrey	Mr. Brian Morrison
Mr. Gord Black	The Family of Roy Muma
Mr. Pat Brown	National Archives of Canada
Mr. Mike Buss	Ontario Archives (Toronto)
Mr. Herb Clark	*The Ottawa Citizen*
Mr. Dino D'Agostini	Ms. Josette Pozzo
Mr. Paul Dennis	Ms. Margaret Reed
The Family of Wilfred Faubert	The Family of Wayne Robinson
Mr. Ken Henry	Mr. Will Samis
Mr. Alfred Hodgson	Mr. Peter Skuce
Ms. Joan Hubay	Mr. Blake Smith
Mr. Ron Jean-Marie	*Sylva Magazine*
Mr. Peter Kataquapit	Mr. Mike Thede
Mr. David Kenney	*The Toronto Star*
Mr. Brad Labadie	Mr. Joel Tost
Mr. John Macfie	Mr. Sanford Trotter
The Family of Neil MacNaughtan	Ms. Marion Weatherhead
Mr. John McDonald	The Family of John Willmott
The Maw Family	Mr. Mervin Windover
	Mr. Mark Woermke

The Warden's Century: A Timetable of Change

1892 The Act for the Protection of Game and Fur-Bearing Animals is enacted.

A chief warden, four part-time field officers and 392 deputy wardens are hired by the Ontario Board of Game and Fish Commissioners under the chairship of Dr. G.A. MacCallum. The wardens—based in Hamilton, Beaumaris, Belleville, Leamington and Dunnville—are paid $10 a month. The deputies are not paid but receive half the fines of any penalties imposed on their evidence.

Thirty thousand copies of the game laws are distributed across Ontario.

1893 Chief warden A.D. Stewart reports that the slaughter of game has been reduced to one-quarter of previous levels.

Ontario is divided into five wardens' zones.

Algonquin Provincial Park, the first provincial park, enacted.

1894 Wardens' annual salaries are increased from $120 to $400.

1896 First resident deer licence ($2) introduced. More than 3,400 are issued.

1898 Ontario wins jurisdiction over provincial fisheries from the federal government.

1899 S.T. Bastedo, deputy commissioner of the Ontario Fisheries Branch, urges the formation of more clubs and associations to aid the government in "the great work of protection."

Rod and Gun in Canada magazine is founded.

The steamer *Gilphie* is purchased for $3,250 and Georgian Bay enforcement is upgraded.

1900 Deputy wardens are required to take an oath of office, binding them to discharge their duties honestly. As a result, their numbers decline from 527 to 209.

1903 The sale of game fish is prohibited, a radical move that saves bass and muskellunge, especially, for sport fishing.

1907   The Department of Game and Fisheries is founded. Seven wardens are based in Simcoe, Windsor, Belleville, Beaumaris, North Bay, Sault Ste. Marie and Kenora.

1911   Annual report of the Department of Game and Fisheries mentions a "widespread system of pollution of our lakes, rivers and streams."

1912   Commissioner Kelly Evans issues a report calling for the complete overhaul of game wardens' administration.

1914   Fur dealers are licensed.

Many wardens leave their jobs to fight in the First World War.

1916   First trapper's licence ($5) is introduced and sealing of pelts inaugurated.

Migratory Birds Convention signed between Canada and the United States for the greater protection of waterfowl.

1917   First Ontario Crown Game Preserve opens in Grey County.

1920   The Department of Game and Fisheries is enlarged to sixty full-time overseers under seven district superintendents.

1921   The Game and Fisheries Department stages its first public exhibit at Toronto's Canadian National Exhibition.

1924   The Ontario Provincial Air Service (O.P.A.S.) takes wing.

Driven by scarcity, beaver and otter harvests are cancelled across southern Ontario.

1926   First gun licence ($1) is issued.

Inaugural meeting of the Toronto Anglers Association takes place. The association later joins the Ontario Federation of Anglers.

1928   A fish culture branch is set up to promote the restocking of lakes and to detect pollution in suspect areas.

1929   Game and Fisheries Act amended to empower wardens to search aircraft.

1930   A special committee on the game-fish situation declares that the field service is "far too small" either to check summer tourists adequately or to protect fish and wildlife.

Wardens' uniforms are introduced.

1931   The Federation of Ontario Naturalists is formed.

1934	Hepburn government announces the firing of 117 wardens and 500 deputies.
	Game and fish violations fall from 810 convictions in 1933 to 491 in 1934, the lowest since records started in 1919.
	Pelee Island is the first of twenty-seven regulated townships for hunting small game. The Pelee Island pheasant shoot is launched with the first regulated township fee.
1938	The province of Ontario stocks more fish than all other provinces and the federal government combined.
1939	Many wardens enlist for the Second World War.
1941	The Ontario Federation of Anglers and Hunters (O.F.A.H.) was formed from the amalgamation of the Ontario Federation of Anglers and the Ontario Hunters' Association.
1946	The Department of Game and Fisheries is incorporated into the Department of Lands and Forests. Wardens are grouped under the Division of Fish and Wildlife, led by Dr. William Harkness.
	Conservation officers—mostly Second World War veterans—first train at Ontario Forest Ranger School, Dorset.
	Dr. Harkness orders all wardens to turn in their revolvers. Months later, the order is reversed and new firearms are issued.
	Ontario Council of Commercial Fisheries is established (later to be renamed the Ontario Fish Producers' Association).
1947	The Ontario Trappers Association is formed.
1948	Wardens or overseers are renamed conservation officers.
	First C.O. presence at the ministry exhibit at the Toronto Sportsmen's Show, later renamed the Outdoor Canada Show.
1949	Fur management officers—later to become wildlife management officers—are introduced.
1954	Ballistics experts are first used in prosecuting fish and wildlife cases.
1957	Hunter Safety Training programme is initiated by Al Young.
1960	Dr. C.H.D. Clarke becomes chief of the Fish and Wildlife Branch.
	Peter Kataquapit is the first aboriginal man to be hired as a C.O.
	Edible "survival" buttons appear on C.O.s' parkas.

1962	The Game and Fisheries Act becomes the Game and Fish Act. A C.O.'s traditional designation as a "constable" is excluded.
1964	A three-week law enforcement course is introduced at the Ontario Police College, Aylmer, for supervisors of C.O.s.
1968	General diploma courses are switched from the Forest Ranger School to Sir Sandford Fleming College, Lindsay.
1971	Bob McGillivray becomes Ontario's first flying enforcement officer.
	The Department of Lands and Forests becomes the Ministry of Natural Resources (M.N.R.).
1976	Ralf Aldrich is appointed as Ontario's first provincial enforcement specialist.
1979	The Minister of Natural Resources directly appoints all deputy conservation officers.
	The Ontario Conservation Officer's Association is formed.
1980	M.N.R. introduces a mandatory trapper education programme.
	Firearms training begins in earnest for all C.O.s who must reach a basic level of marksmanship in yearly shoots.
	Margaret Reed of Chatham District is appointed the first female C.O.
	Community Fisheries Involvement Program (C.F.I.P.) is introduced.
1982	The Charter of Rights and Freedoms and subsequent human rights directives modify the C.O.s' basic job requirements concerning height, weight, age and a grade 12 education.
	The Charter of Rights and Freedoms recognizes aboriginal and treaty rights.
1983	C.O. marksmanship awards are introduced.
1985	Community Wildlife Involvement Program (C.W.I.P.) and Project WILD are inaugurated.
1986	Special Investigations Unit is formally established.
	Ontario resident's fishing licence is introduced.
1987	The Kenrick Report maintains that the greatest advancement in the evolution of C.O.s over the past decade has been "the enhancement of enforcement training."

A Timetable of Change

1988 M.N.R. makes available batons and bulletproof vests for C.O.s.

C.O. Ted Biggs begins training for twenty-two firearms instructors across the province.

1989 More than 300 people apply for a bilingual C.O.'s position in Algonquin Park.

Timmins is the first city to launch a Report-A-Poacher programme in conjunction with Crime Stoppers International.

More than 100 officers march on Queen's Park in pay and classification protest.

1990 Ontario's C.O.s win a $11 million settlement making them the third highest paid wardens in North America.

C.O. Ian Anderson is awarded the International Game Warden Fraternalism Award for his leadership and advice on professional issues in Ontario and in other provinces and states.

1991 A Sudbury court accepts for the first time in North America the validity of D.N.A. fingerprinting in a poaching trial.

Pilot canine programme is launched in Sudbury.

A new Compliance Policy Branch is established with the appointment of Andy Houser as director.

Glossary of Terms

Bag census

A bag census is similar to a creel census (see below), but is used for land animals, e.g., partridges and grouse. The bag census checks for possession or legal limits.

Blackjack

Blackjacks are billies that used to be carried by C.O.s, and are usually about seventeen to twenty centimetres long. They have a spring inside them and a lead ball on the end. Blackjacks are no longer considered an acceptable or suitable self-defence weapon.

C.F.I.P.

Community Fisheries Involvement Program is a Ministry of Natural Resources programme encouraging individuals and groups to carry on fisheries projects with the assistance of the M.N.R.

Creel census

Creel census is a multi-purpose survey of fish and commercial fishers/anglers. The biological aspect of the creel census provides such information as type, weight and length of fish, as well as scale samples used to confirm the age of the fish. This information may be used to determine which years were successful for fish development.

Also included in a creel census may be information about where the commercial fisher/angler is from, and in which portion of the lake fish are being caught the most.

C.W.I.P.

Community Wildlife Involvement Program is a Ministry of Natural Resources programme encouraging individuals and groups to carry on wildlife projects with the assistance of the M.N.R.

Fry

Fry refers to young fish, newly hatched, after the yolk has been used up and active feeding has commenced.

Fingerling

Fingerling refers to young fish, usually late in first year.

Glossary

Gill net

Gill net is a type of fish net that traps the fish by its gills.

Goose hunting camps

Goose hunting camps are run by First Nation people in Moosonee. Operators take non-native hunters to the camps around Hudson Bay and James Bay.

Jacklighting

Jacklighting is an illegal method of shooting deer at night. Hunters daze deer with powerful spotlights and make them a stationary target.

"Pinch" books

A term used by C.O.s to describe their ticket books where they keep their tickets, receipts, notes, etc.

Punt

A punt is a little boat used for duck hunting in marshes. Traditionally, it is a flat-bottom boat no longer than four metres.

Sealing Furs

Seals for furs were similar to boxcar seals; they were put through the eyes of a fur. The seals had numbers on them, enabling them to be traced back to where the fur was sealed and who owned the fur. Nowadays, an ink stamp is used for the same purpose.

Seine

A seine is a type of long net that is dragged along the bottom of a river. When the two ends are drawn together, the seine encloses the fish in the centre of a circle. Usually the net is ten to twenty metres long with weights fastened to the bottom and floats fastened on the top.

Snagging

Snagging is an illegal method of fishing in which a hook is used to catch the fish in areas other than the mouth, for example, the back or tail.

Transects

Transect lines are flight lines an airplane will fly and take animal sightings from (commonly used for moose surveys). An airplane takes a bearing and flies a straight line.